Awake, Not Woke

Awake, Not Woke

"Noelle Mering pierces the dark heart of wokery, and, with her characteristically engaging and often funny prose, sheds bright light on matters notorious for their heat. This is the field manual of bad ideas we have been waiting for. Highly recommended."

—Patrick Coffin, Author and Co-founder, CoffinNation.com

"Noelle Mering's *Awake, Not Woke* is essential reading to understand the dominant views of social justice today. It is an engaging and serious book that distills the animating principles of the "woke" movement, and explains the intellectual history behind it. But Mering doesn't stop at critical analysis. She takes seriously the claims and grievances of racism, injustice, and abuse and offers a response rooted not in power and conflict, but in deep interpersonal relationships and the human need to live in truth and to be known and loved."

—Michael Miller, Senior Research Fellow at the Acton Institute and Director and Producer of *Poverty Inc.*

"*Awake, Not Woke* presents a clear and crushing critique of an ideology that is at this very moment poisoning our culture. With tremendous skill, wit, understanding, and compassion, Noelle Mering traces the historical roots of wokism, its dogmas and methods of indoctrination, and its heart-breaking fruits. She also identifies the path to restoration. How I wish every American could read this book!"

—Kenneth Hensley, co-author of *The Godless Delusion* and host of *On the Journey* show and podcast

"A powerful pseudo-religious movement now threatens the very survival of Christianity in the west. Christians and their leaders not only refuse to confront this dangerous political and cultural revolution, but increasingly embrace its destructive heresies. Others realize they are under attack but are confused about why and what to do about it. Noelle Mering is the brave, insightful, and vital prophetic voice they desperately need to understand what is happening, and how to counter it. She elegantly exposes this movement for what it is. All Christians—and anyone seeking to understand what is now happening in America—need to read it."

—Matthew J. Peterson, Founding Editor of *The American Mind* and Vice President of Education at The Claremont Institute

"*Awake, Not Woke* is an invaluable resource for today's cultural confusion. Mering deftly sifts through the jargon to understand, explain, and refute, the current state of the Progressive movement. Though analyzed in a Christian context, much of the weight of the argument is grounded in universal principles of human nature. It's a book driven less by politics and more for the care for people and concern for the wide and lasting harm of a dehumanizing ideology."

—Carrie Gress, Author of *The Anti-Mary Exposed* and *Theology of Home*

AWAKE, NOT WOKE

A Christian Response to the Cult of Progressive Ideology

Noelle Mering

TAN Books
Gastonia, North Carolina

Cover design by Wesley Bancroft

Cover image: Painting of Jesus Christ in the Sacred Sacristy Museum in St Katherine Monastery on the Sinai Peninsula in Egypt, bimages / Alamy Stock Photo

Library of Congress Control Number: 2021931591

ISBN: 978-1-5051-1842-1
Kindle ISBN: 978-1-5051-1843-8
ePUB ISBN: 978-1-5051-1844-5

Published in the United States by
TAN Books
PO Box 269
Gastonia, NC 28053
www.TANBooks.com

Printed in the United States of America

To Fr. Paul Donlan, who has been a gentle but truly powerful instrument of the Holy Spirit in my life

"Awake, O sleeper, and arise from the dead, and Christ shall give you light."

—Ephesians 5:14

Contents

Acknowledgments

I am grateful to so many wonderful friends and family members who have offered support for this book along the way. Some generous souls provided invaluable assistance, including Carrie Gress, Alex Lessard, Jon Kirwan, and Nancy Mering.

Family members Nicole and Ray Tittmann and Irene and Phillip Cronin were wonderful sounding boards and support throughout.

Special thanks to the team at TAN Books, especially Brian Kennelly and Conor Gallagher, for their encouragement, professionalism, and talent. And to Wesley Marc Bancroft for an inspired cover design.

I am grateful to those who have published my articles, some of which ended up in partial form here: Kevin Knight at *National Catholic Register*, Joy Pullmann at *The Federalist*, and Matthew Peterson at *The American Mind*.

Most especially, my family—my heroic husband, Adam, and our dear children Abby, Jack, Campion, Caroline, Vivienne, and Vera—who have sacrificed for and supported this effort with an immense amount of love and accommodation.

Introduction

The battle for word and meaning that grips our nation is dramatically played out every spring in a wealthy suburb west of Boston. In an account relayed by the *New York Times*, at the end of the school year, Wellesley College holds a commencement service during which students, faculty, and guests come together to sing "America the Beautiful." Recently, as the crowd came to the line, "And crown thy good with . . ." parents and guests proceeded to sing *brotherhood*, the word that was originally intended to include women too. Wellesley women, however, had adopted the custom in past decades of abruptly belting out *sisterhood*, drowning out the word that they felt oppressively excluded them and replacing it with a demand for recognition. Journalist Ruth Padawer writes, "It's one of the most powerful moments of commencement, followed every year by cheers, applause and tears, evoked by the rush of solidarity with women throughout time, and the thrill of claiming in one of the nation's most famous songs that women matter—even if the world they're about to enter doesn't always agree."

Padawer goes on to say that over the last few years, some graduates have taken it upon themselves to change that word once again, determining that *sisterhood*, while a well-intended change, is still exclusionary. Instead, they sing *siblinghood*. Padawer continues, "A few trans men find even that insufficient, and in that instant, they roar the word that represents them best: 'brotherhood,' not as a sexist stand-in for all humankind, but as an appeal from a tiny minority struggling to be acknowledged."

In perhaps the most revealing description of the event, Padawer writes, "In truth, it's difficult to distinguish in the cacophony each of the words shouted atop one another. What is clear is that whatever word each person is hollering is immensely significant as a proclamation of existence, even if it's hard to make out what anyone else is saying."[1]

Hardly just ceremonial end-of-year activism, this sort of drama at Wellesley is commonplace on the historically all-female campus. On a recent fall day, a new student began to request she be referred to by male pronouns despite the fact that she had applied as a woman and that she was indeed a woman. She now identified as "masculine-of-center gender-queer." This was not particularly shocking to her peers, as there were other transgender students on campus. Timothy (as she asked to be called) was accommodated and affirmed easily by the far-left school culture. The problem arose when Timothy decided to run for a student leadership role as coordinator of multicultural affairs. The job was to promote a "culture of diversity" on campus. Students, though generally friendly with Timothy, began to object that she, as a "white man," was not representative of the diversity such a role required. Students coordinated an online campaign

<hr>

[1] Ruth Padawer, "When Women Become Men at Wellesley," New York Times, October 15, 2014, https://www.nytimes.com/2014/10/19/magazine/when-women-become-men-at-wellesley-college.html.

to reject Timothy based on the understanding that a "white man" in leadership would perpetuate the patriarchy. When asked how she felt, Timothy confessed to feeling conflicted. She believed herself to be a minority as a trans student but also knew that the patriarchy was alive and well and did not want to be part of the perpetuation of oppression.

The importance of language on popular thought can be overstated as much as it can be underestimated. Words today are considered to be acts of violence, and yet malleable enough for us to manipulate in service of our preferred agenda. Either way, they are a sort of weapon—threatening to wound us in our nebulous sense of self, or else a type of revolutionary shot fired—a proclamation of our existence against a world against us. Each of us is ruler of his own constitutive reality—distrustful but needy, fragile but hot-tempered.

A breakdown in our common understanding of words leads to a society in chaos and frustration, inevitably miscommunicating and plagued by distrust. We become suspicious, not only of each other, but of ourselves and our ability to grasp reality. Rather than a fallible people struggling imperfectly toward a harmonious common good, we are a cacophony screaming across a chasm for recognition and moving through the world without a destination.

In his book *The Beginning of Wisdom*, Leon Kass writes of the breakdown of common language at the Tower of Babel. "And because language also bespeaks the inner world of the speakers, sharing one language means also a common inner life, with simple words accurately conveying the selfsame imaginings, passions, and desires of every human being. To be 'of one language' is to be of one mind and heart about the most fundamental things."[2]

When our shared language becomes compromised, we lose not only the utility of it, which enables us to convey basic facts about the practical realities of daily life, but also any common and universal meaning toward which our daily lives and our interior lives might point.

It does not take much convincing to see our society as it currently stands is experiencing this crisis of meaning, not just in the form of communication or means, but also about ends and purposes—our understanding of which indicates and informs our understanding of everything else. Increasingly, this crisis not only threatens the relationship between Christians and secularists but fractures Christian communities from within. Christian community life depends on the interior life of each believer. In disorienting our hidden life, we exponentially fracture our communal life.

We cannot build any tower, even were it not a doomed hubristic enterprise, because we are arguing over the building blocks. Consider how drastically we have altered the meaning and usage of simple words like *love, hate, man, woman,* and *marriage.* Consider the new vocabulary that we have introduced into our cultural psyche (the day before yesterday): words such as *white privilege, intersectionality, cisgender, heteronormativity,* and *positionality.* Not only are such concepts suddenly everywhere, but conformity to their proper use is increasingly demanded. But it is not just the

---

[2]   Leon Kass, *The Beginning of Wisdom* (University of Chicago Press, 2006), p. 223.

building blocks that are corrupted; the purpose of the project is obscured entirely.

Of this, George Orwell writes:

> Now, it is clear that the decline of a language must ultimately have political and economic causes: it is not due simply to the bad influence of this or that individual writer. But an effect can become a cause, reinforcing the original cause and producing the same effect in an intensified form, and so on indefinitely. A man may take to drink because he feels himself to be a failure, and then fail all the more completely because he drinks. It is rather the same thing that is happening to the English language. It becomes ugly and inaccurate because our thoughts are foolish, but the slovenliness of our language makes it easier for us to have foolish thoughts. The point is that the process is reversible.[3]

Far from a peevish culture war, this is an attempt to revolutionize the way in which we see the world in and around us and the meaning imbued within those realities. Once we cease to see words as having a power to reveal reality, they are reduced to reflections not of reality but of ourselves. Rather than a bridge of communication, we are left with a staircase to nowhere as words become unintelligible altogether.

---

[3] George Orwell, "Politics and the English Language," Orwell.ru, Accessed June 10, 2020, https://www.orwell.ru/library/essays/politics/english/e_polit.

Love and Truth

A casualty of this manipulation of language is the concept of truth itself. There is a facile tendency to pit truth and love against one another. While it is a false dichotomy in principle, it is easy to imagine all sorts of practical examples in which an insipid admonition such as "it is better to be kind than right" might actually be useful. When a woman asks her husband how she looks, the material truth might be that she looks tired, or older, or has gained some weight, or is wearing an unflattering color. These things ought not be said, and so in demurring and saying she looks beautiful, a husband is, in a way, preferring love to truth. But in a deeper way, he is speaking a fuller truth: that her beauty is not limited to a physical or scientific examination of her bodily attributes or the aesthetics of her attire but that there is a real way in which one's beauty takes into account the entirety of the person. The spirit or soul of an individual even becomes manifest in her physically—the wisdom in her eyes, the levity in her expression, the body that bears the mark of their life and love together.

The dichotomy which pits love against truth is also commonly used to avoid or delay difficult realities in an effort to spare the feelings of another. We can easily imagine how this is defensible advice in certain circumstances. Even if he is correct, a Christian ought not be a pedantic scold going around pointing out the error in the thoughts or actions of others. To do so might be to speak something true, but it would be imprudent and unloving. Furthermore, a society long accustomed to watching shadows on the cave wall must be led gradually, yet resolutely, into the light. St. Paul speaks of this: "I fed you with milk, not solid food; for you were not ready for it" (1 Cor. 3:2). Truth must be balanced with prudence and charity.

If either of these examples were all that is meant by the admonition that it is better to be kind than right, then it would be fine and even helpful advice. But the admonition to censor hard truths under the guise of kindness has gone far beyond curbing the scold or safeguarding a marriage. Rather, what is often intended is the elimination of such teachings altogether.

What *should not* be said soon becomes what *cannot* be said, either due to the force of law or the demagoguery of political correctness. With a semblance of love, truth is soon abandoned altogether. The weakness of most Christians today is not that we are too strident but that we are too cowardly.

"The modern world is full of the old Christian virtues gone mad," writes Chesterton. "The virtues have gone mad because they have been isolated from each other and are wandering alone. Thus some scientists care for truth; and their truth is pitiless. Thus some humanitarians only care for pity; and their pity (I am sorry to say) is often untruthful."[4] Isolated from one another, each virtue ceases to even be itself.

---

[4]   G. K. Chesterton, *Orthodoxy* (Dover Publications, INC, 2004), p. 22.

The Word

Though truth is now commonly subjugated under the pretense of an appeal to compassion or with the intimidation of societal shaming, for the Christian, no such dichotomy can exist. In losing a moral vocabulary, we lose the ability to name what is wounding us. In acquiescing to these categories which seek to pit love against truth, Christians lose an understanding not only of how we ought to live but *why* we ought to live.

The capacity to speak the truth is intimately tied to our freedom to live meaningful lives. When a student is brought before the headmaster at my children's school for some misbehavior, he sometimes asks the student to tell him the story of Rumpelstiltskin. In this story, a princess has made a deal out of desperation with an unnamed creature who came to her aid. In exchange for some of his magical power to spin yarn into gold, she must give him her future firstborn child. Her only chance to escape this pact is to discover the creature's name. In contemplating this story, the student is taught the lesson that we must look with sincerity at ourselves and our situation and we must speak it. We have to name a thing in order to be free of it. "The unnameable is far more terrifying than the nameable," says Jordan Peterson.[5]

This book is an attempt to name what is poisoning us. In order to do that, we have to understand the history, premises, and tactics of woke ideology, which is fundamentally

---

[5]   Jordan Peterson, "Rule 10: Be Precise in Your Speech," from an interview with The Rubin Report streamed live on November 1, 2017, YouTube video, https://www.youtube.com/watch?v=d3k tWt8r5Eg.

an ideology of rupture. The term *woke* refers to the state of being alert and attuned to the layers of pervasive oppression in society. While it originated specifically with regard to racism, it has since broadened to include all areas of social oppression commonly considered to be along the lines of gender, race, and sexuality. Specific acts of injustice are used to serve the larger goal of furthering the ideology that sees all of human interaction as a power contest. Growth for the woke movement is measured by fracturing. Indeed, it is an ideology with fundamentalist and even cult-like characteristics that is on a collision course with Christianity.

It is not only destructive but incoherent. It is a war of words against the Word. It is a revolution which elevates will over reason, the group over the person, and human power over higher authority. What is rejected—reason, the person, and authority—are the three characteristics of the Logos himself. The Logos is the *mind* of God, communicated in the *person* of Jesus Christ, who is the author of all and *authority* over all. Whether explicitly or not, he is the ultimate target of the woke revolt.

It is a revolt that manifests itself in various ways in every age, and one which St. John knew in his day. "In the beginning was the Word, and the Word was with God, and the Word was God. He was in the beginning with God; all things were made through him, and without him was not anything made that was made" (Jn 1:1–3). "And the word became flesh." God, the logos, the word, is being itself. He is "Who am." Where the very nature of God is ordered, unitive, and generative, the spirit of this counter movement is at its core the very nature of the devil: chaotic, divisive, sterile.

While woke ideology appears as a benevolent fight for justice, it is far from that. It lures us in with an appeal to our better natures, then replaces intelligible principles with distorted ones, resulting in incoherence and chaos. What if under the guise of eradicating bigotry, we have entrenched it? What if in trying to coexist, we have siloed ourselves into warring tribes? What if where once there was civic friendship, we have introduced resentment and division? What if in undermining the source of authority, we have imprisoned ourselves in an endless scramble for power?

While it is easy to dismiss wokeness as being a movement on the fringe or "out there," to do so would be shortsighted. We are called to engage with the world in which we find ourselves. To write off a growing phenomenon which is both affecting and reflecting real persons is to shirk that duty of engagement. Charity demands that we make a real effort to understand, rather than just hold in contempt, the people falling prey to this ideology. People are looking for meaning in their lives and answers to human questions such as why we are here and how we ought to live. If we aren't providing these answers in a compelling way, they won't remain unanswered; they will be answered in distorted half-truths that promise but cannot deliver real solutions.

With the hubris of trying to erect a utopian tower, we labor in vain, having cut ourselves off from the means and the ends. With the moral chaos of greater liberation comes a prison of negotiation. Instead of a ballet of true freedom born of discipline, we have contracts born of vulnerability and suspicion. "For socialism is not only the labor question . . . but first of all the question of atheism, the question of the modern embodiment of atheism, the question of the tower of Babel built precisely without God, not to go from earth to heaven, but to bring heaven down to earth."[6]

Woke ideology has crept and dripped like a poison into corners and cells of an unsuspecting body of people. It corrupts Christianity by turning it into a religion without justice, without mercy, and ultimately without Christ. The stakes could not be higher. Let's begin naming it.

---

[6]   Fyodor Dostoevsky, *The Brothers Karamazov* (Farrar, Straus and Giroux, 2002), p. 26.

PART I

Origins

Ye Shall Be as Gods

"Two cities were created by two loves. The earthly city was created by self-love reaching the point of contempt for God. In the Heavenly City, by the love of God carried as far as contempt for self."[1]

When he wrote *City of God*, St. Augustine knew well what it was to be a citizen in the City of Man. His was a life with shadows and light, knowing an abyss of sin and through that knowledge finding the ineffable mercy of a Savior. His turning back to God, after having chained himself to sin, was finally prompted when, while sitting under a fig tree, he heard a child's voice saying, "Take up and read." He opened Sacred Scripture and read, "The night is far gone, the day is at hand. Let us then cast off the works of darkness and put on the armor of light" (Rom 13:12).

Nine months later, he was baptized. He wrote of his conversion, "All my empty dreams suddenly lost their charm and my heart began to throb with a bewildering passion for the wisdom of eternal truth."[2] His life and writings have been studied, meditated upon, and written about for

---

[1] St. Augustine, *The City of God*, Book 14, Ch. 28.
[2] St. Augustine, *Confessions*, III, 4.

centuries not just because of his writing mastery but due to the enduring relevance of the deeply human and distinctly supernatural themes of sin, struggle, and redemption. These themes are not unique to him but are at stake in the life of every fallen person.

Concerning St. Augustine, sin, and struggle, woke celebrity Lutheran pastor Nadia Bolz-Weber says, "When it came to his ideas around sex and gender, he basically took a dump and the church encased it in amber."[3] In her latest book, *Shameless*, Bolz-Weber calls for a Christian sexual revolution with regard to sex, gender, transgenderism, and feminism. According to her, the effort to deny sexual pleasure in any but the most extreme circumstances is futile, even contrary to God's will.

This belief was crystalized (or encased in amber) for Bolz-Weber when, after leaving a husband with whom she'd found insufficient sexual satisfaction, she began having the gratifying sex she sought with an old boyfriend. She was not under a fig tree, and she heard no angelic voice, but she did have what she describes as a reawakening. "It was like an exfoliant."[4] Through this experience, it became clear to her that Christians needed to reconstruct the moral architecture surrounding sexuality. Bolz-Weber practices what she preaches; when her sixteen-year-old son came to her to say

---

[3]   Eliza Griswold, "The Lutheran Pastor Calling for a Sexual Reformation," *The New Yorker*, February 8, 2019, https://www.newyorker.com/news/on-religion/the-lutheran-pastor-calling-for-a-sexual-reformation.

[4]   Ibid.

he was in a relationship with another boy, she responded by tossing him a pack of condoms.

Nadia Bolz-Weber might seem like an extreme example of the influence of woke culture in Christianity. But while the number of Christians who count themselves among such ranks is small, her embrace of politically correct secular agendas has provided her a platform. *Shameless* is a *New York Times* best seller, with a glowing endorsement from the late and relatively more mainstream Christian figure Rachel Held-Evans. The ceiling for her extreme presentation of woke Christianity might be low, but there are an increasing number of similarly insidious messages presented with less edgy packaging, and spasms of woke protests have been percolating around various Catholic and Protestant colleges with greater frequency.

Much of woke Christianity is framed as a reaction to the ills of traditional Christianity. There is hypocrisy, and harshness, and scandal they say, and, well, the solution just might be to become a faith defined by its reaction to, and rejection of, all of that—to become a kinder, gentler Christianity that is a friend rather than a challenge to the world.

That too many for too long have been raised with a pale and impoverished witness to the richness of Christianity is undeniable. The reality of imperfect people—whose faith is weak, understanding is limited, and love is small—bringing scandal to the faith is nothing new. In fact, that can describe most of us at different times. We can present a proud or harsh or hostile Christianity because we are proud or harsh or hostile.

Additionally, too many for too long have experienced not only a weak presentation of the faith but a perverse one. Abuse happens in every segment of society, but there is something exponentially destructive when it is coupled with a costume of Christianity.

But if we have suffered from infidelity to Christ, we won't resolve that by a different sort of infidelity to him. More holiness, not less, is what is needed. A religion that too closely identifies happiness with the fulfillment of desire will not conceive of anything worth suffering for. A Christianity which averts its eyes to the pervasiveness of sin will not feel the need for an abundance of grace.

Pope Emeritus Benedict XVI spoke to this prior to his papacy in a radio address in 1969:

> The future of the Church, once again as always, will be reshaped by saints, by men, that is, whose minds probe deeper than the slogans of the day, who see more than others see, because their lives embrace a wider reality. Unselfishness, which makes men free, is attained only through the patience of small daily acts of self-denial. By this daily passion, which alone reveals to a man in how many ways he is enslaved by his own ego, by this daily passion and by it alone, a man's eyes are slowly opened. He sees only to the extent that he has lived and suffered. If today we are scarcely able any longer to become aware of God, that is because we find it so easy to evade ourselves, to flee from the depths of our being

by means of the narcotic of some pleasure or other.
Thus our own interior depths remain closed to us.[5]

We have grown blind to this great drama, oblivious to our spiritual poverty. Without knowing our need, our solutions seem merely sentimental. And therein lies the fundamental incoherence of woke Christianity: in seeking to offer the world a veneer of compassion, it robs that world of mercy. We become, as Cardinal George put it, a world that permits everything and forgives nothing—a world that is not only merciless but Christ-less.

The Struggle

Though it is tempting to confine woke ideology in terms of partisan politics, the crisis we face extends far beyond that. This is a spiritual and religious struggle with origins reaching back to a snake in a garden cajoling the first woman that "ye shall be as gods." Behind every temptation to sin is this sales pitch: that we might, in trading our greatest good for various lesser goods, become autonomous, self-determining, powerful. Time and again we are reminded in history and in our personal pursuits that in falling for this promise, we expose it as a lie. Rather than powerful, autonomous, and self-determining, we become small, chaotic, and slaves to ego and impulse. We become weak.

---

[5] Billy Ryan, "The Lost Prophecy of Father Joseph Ratzinger on the Future of the Church," uCatholic, July 24, 2017, https://ucatholic .com/blog/the-lost-prophecy-of-father-joseph-ratzinger-on-the -future-of-the-church/.

This is both old and new. It is a struggle that no one can escape in this life. But something has changed in our understanding of this struggle, and this change has become pervasive and loud. We have ceased to see this struggle as one worth fighting. Increasingly, *we see our good as identical to our desire.* We look suspiciously at references to sin, evil, and hell. Those words are for something "out there" or from long ago, if they even mean anything at all.

More and more we conceive of God as less and less—until he becomes little more than an extension of ourselves or a therapeutic being who serves to comfort and affirm us. "He must decrease, we must increase" is our modern mantra.

Virtue is difficult enough to attain, but it becomes impossible when it is no longer seen as a goal worthy of pursuit. The struggle to do the good predates Christianity and exists in its most synthesized ancient form in the writings of Aristotle, who said that to be a rational animal and to live a fully human life is to do the good habitually. Such habits train us to delight in the self-mastery and the freedom that virtue introduces. But as long as we live, there will always be a pull to swim downstream.

St. Paul speaks of the struggle, "But I see in my members another law at war with the law of my mind and making me captive to the law of sin which dwells in my members" (Rom 7:23). Instead, we have shifted the locus of the struggle from internal to external. Aleksander Solzhenitsyn was a man who knew the depths of evil, having endured eight years imprisoned in a labor camp for the crime of having criticized communism. Still, he famously wrote in *The Gulag Archipelago*, "If only it were all so simple! If only there were evil people somewhere insidiously committing evil deeds, and it were necessary only to separate them from the rest of us and destroy them. But the line dividing good and evil cuts through the heart of every human being."

Two Cities

Though its roots and history are atheistic, woke ideology takes on the manner and characteristics of a fundamentalist religion. It has its dogmas and denunciations. It replaces the struggle against sin with struggle sessions. Its vision is messianic, its dogmas unquestionable. But rather than an eternal end, it finds and administers salvation and damnation in *this* world. As it co-opts the culture, it co-opts Christians, but it does so parasitically. Woke Christianity, if such a thing might be said to exist at all, will inevitably reject Christ in all but name.

A stage is set for a collision between an illusory god of self and the one true God. In principle, woke ideology establishes a modern incarnation of the City of Man, not because it is the wrong politics, but because it allows nothing but politics. It crowds out any vision of the eternal city and instead reduces the world to a decrepit mansion with mirrors and facades and the embers of an old fire.

The two cities do not have a visible demarcation line; they remain intermingled in this life. Each city—of God and of man—is constituted with doctrines, dogmas, rites, codes, and evangelistic zeal. Citizens in either can be kind or cruel, and citizenship can move from one city to the other (and back again). But while one points its citizens to eternity and the glory of God, the other seeks only the goods of this world and the glory of self.

Shy away from it as we might, death is not an if but a when. And the four last things—death, judgment, heaven, hell—that come when we open our eyes on the other side concern things not of a moment but of an eternity.

Writhing and thrashing against this hope of eternal beatitude is the same serpent let loose in this post-Eden carnival. Serpents are believed to symbolize many things, but our conception of the serpent's basic nature has remained relatively consistent; it is androgynous—both phallic and feminine. They are cunning and voracious—all intellect and appetite. In this way, they are an icon of what C. S. Lewis called "men without chests," creatures who know the good but have no love or affection for it, and so instead are crafty and self-indulgent.

Leon Kass, in his analysis of Genesis, says the serpent is an "embodiment of the separated and beguiling voice of autonomous human reason speaking up against innocence and obedience, coming to us as if from some attractive force outside us that whispers doubt into our ears. In making his rationalist mischief, speech is the serpent's only weapon."[6]

In the garden, and in each of our lives, the serpent whispers to us that we might be as gods. He does not approach us asking us to fall down and worship him initially, nor does he entice Eve to him by explicitly undermining God. Instead, he implies that God is reduced, just one of many goods, and

---

[6]   Leon Kass, *The Beginning of Wisdom* (University of Chicago Press, 2006), p. 82.

certainly not to be preferred above all else. The serpent is cunning.

Lewis wisely gleaned the meaning and importance of men with chests. "It may even be said that it is by this middle element that man is man: for by his intellect he is mere spirit and by his appetite mere animal."[7] Lewis determines that it is through trained affections that we delight in what pleases God and disdain what separates us from him. It is the chest—the heart—that provides the connective tissue between the other two organs of mind and stomach (reason and appetite), enabling us to not just know the good but to desire it. It is what the childhood story of *Madeline* refers to with the simple line that the children smiled at the good and frowned at the bad, not as a posture, but from a true and ordered harmony of soul that has come to see the good and desire it.

A Crisis of Meaning

It is this heart of man that cannot be satiated with what is on offer from ideology. A college professor, Ian Corbin, wrote of a hopeful, if anecdotal, encounter speaking to two graduating seniors, one man and one woman, both progressive activists, and neither white.

> They shared one particular frustration, perhaps the opposite of what one would think. Both said they had felt constrained in their time at BC by certain norms of speech and thought, especially around topics like

---

[7] C. S. Lewis, *The Abolition of Man* (Collier Books, Macmillan Publishing Company, 1947), p. 34.

gender, relationships, race, etc. Both felt pressured to adopt certain progressive certainties that papered over the texture of an actual human life. Both of them assumed that this was due to some very strange particularities of their own lives—an idiosyncratic desire, for instance, to find a husband and raise children, a weird experience of women and men as being different from one another, in ways that might be relevant for the conduct of romantic relationships.[8]

There are true ideologues, faithful to the woke dogmas. But there is also a quiet, but likely not small, subset of people who are repeating a script, with little heart, as they are quietly pulled by design and desire to the possibility of deep meaning and the hope of some grand fulfillment of an unidentified longing. Parroting woke indignance in all the correct ways by all the old things becomes tedious and thin. Everything bores us and we grow dependent on our outrage as the only emotion that we are able to access. In a carnival of pleasures, we don't have an architecture of meaning. These are shallow but tumultuous waters to wade through. Passions are sharp and consuming. Because we don't know how to suffer well, we suffer loudly. We are drowning in puddles when we should be learning to swim in oceans.

In speaking about this, Viktor Frankl contrasts the lack of neurosis and suicidal thoughts among prisoners in Auschwitz with the growing phenomenon of suicidal thoughts from teens living with ease in modern Austria. "We are

---

[8]   Ian Marcus Corbin, "Losing the Class," *The American Mind*, July 19, 2019, https://americanmind.org/essays/losing-the-class/.

living in a society, either in terms of an affluent society or in terms of a welfare state. . . . These types of societies are out to satisfy and gratify each and every human need. Except for one need, the most basic and fundamental need . . . the need for meaning."[9] Suffering is intimately tied to meaning. Serial gratification is intimately bound up with despair.

The suppression of meaning is the deepest form of oppression and slavery that human beings can exact upon one another. In contrast, the fear of the repression of our desires by a demanding God has little to do with the lived experience of deep friendship with Christ. It is this friendship that allowed St. Maximillian Kolbe to give his life freely and with joy for the sake of another prisoner in Auschwitz. It is this friendship that enabled Cardinal Văn Thuận, imprisoned in solitary confinement by the Communist regime, to see his prison as his cathedral and move his guards to the point of their conversion to the faith. It is this friendship that is profoundly liberating, not with the scant liberty of licentiousness, but with the true freedom of an eternal family.

While woke culture is in many ways born of a decadent time, we always run the risk—and in 2020 it seemed the sudden reality—that the trappings of decadence will be stripped away with war, pandemic, riots, or natural disaster. Introduced into the void left behind will be something, be it a deep religious revival of meaning or something more sinister in the guise of a solution. The tension between those two

---

9   Viktor Frankl, "Viktor Frankl: Youngsters need challenges," YouTube video posted by Noetic Films, July 2, 2019, original video from 1979, https://www.youtube.com/watch?v=ImonPWt7VOA.

options is a battle fought both within societies and within the heart of each person.

The promise that we can cut ourselves off from the Almighty and have no master has been disproven time and again, but still it is seeded and sown in new generations, the woke being our current iteration. As Bob Dylan said, "You're gonna have to serve somebody." In the City of Man, absent true authority, a tyrant-master always rises to grasp power.

2

The Road to Frankfurt

Within the umbrella of the woke ideology, there tend to be two types of people: the well-intended, who seek justice but misunderstand the real aims of the movement, and the militant true believers. Though the militant are fewer, they are in many ways directing the movement and are the ones willing to play out the internal violent logic of the ideology.

To grasp that logic, we need to know its history, especially in the Frankfurt School, a research center which began as the Institute for Social Research—an adjunct of Goethe University in Frankfurt—with the aim of developing and promulgating Marxism in Germany. The Frankfurt School (as it came to be known) moved to New York City in 1935, bringing with it the dramatic convergence of Marxist philosophy, Freudian psychology, rank perversion, and all manner of lurid ideas and practices introduced for the destruction and dismantling of Western culture by way of the destruction and dismantling of the family. Marxism and social theorists at the Frankfurt School are often dismissed as marginally influential, existing only in the insular far-away world of left-wing academia, where its dictates are forgotten as quickly as

27

they are learned. On the contrary, these ideas have become deeply ingrained, not just in the universities, but now in the culture and media. Because many have uncritically absorbed their dogmas, it's essential that we grapple with their meaning and history.

Hegel, Dialectic, and Consciousness

Karl Marx was a nineteenth-century German political theorist writing in the wake of the Industrial Revolution. He, along with many of his contemporaries, was devoted to the writings of German philosopher George Hegel (1770–1831) and captivated by Hegel's new way of thinking about history. The convergence of the philosophies of Hegel and Marx with regard to historical development and progress would become the bedrocks of the Frankfurt School.

Hegel believed that all events and ideas are expressions of the spirit of a culture and that, through a process of internal tensions and resolutions, societies work through time toward an idealized, elevated cultural consciousness. Ideas interact with each other and evolve, not randomly, but toward a goal of complete cultural self-determination or self-realization through the development of mind and understanding. The process by which this development toward an ideal state occurs is what Hegel called the dialectic.

The dialectic laid the groundwork for the Progressive understanding of history—that through a series of conflicts and resolutions, societies progress toward a more perfected state. It was in this framework of dialectic that Marx found the groundwork to justify and advance a total break with the past and the seeds of a revolutionary transformation of the future.

According to Hegelian dialectic, within every society and at any given time there is a status quo, or norm of circumstances and thought, that we tend to accept as products of our time. This status quo is what Hegel called the thesis (the way things are). Though the status quo can seem relatively harmonious, this stage always has conflicting internal elements, seeds that will cause it to break down as internal conflicts are realized through individual consciousness. The next stage is the growing awareness of, and agitation about, the internal conflict within the status quo, eventually leading to a revolt against the thesis. This stage is called the antithesis (the conflicting interest). The third stage is the synthesis: the result of the conflict between the thesis and the antithesis is the new order of things. Synthesis will have its own internal conflicts, and so it becomes the new thesis, and the process repeats itself. A tyrant might rule a state (thesis) until those under his rule realize their oppression and revolt (antithesis). They achieve a measure of freedom (synthesis) and begin the next stage of status quo (thesis).

Hegel used the French Revolution as an example. First came the revolt against the French monarchy, which, during the Reign of Terror, included massacres and public executions in a glut of rage and revolution. After the Reign of Terror, there followed a constitutional society that seemingly better valued the rights of individual citizens. Each stage played a necessary role in the progress of history, justifying whatever violent means got them there. Guillotines, terror, and the bloodshed of innocents are justified for the sake of the progress of history through which a societal transformation of consciousness makes a god of the collective.[1]

Conflict Theory

As a young man, Karl Marx became an apologist and evangelist for Hegelianism. Marx seized on the dialectic framework as a way to stoke a societal consciousness toward endless critique and crisis—what he called conflict theory. But Marx made an important shift. Hegel, having already rejected the notion of a Judeo-Christian God, saw the dialectic as aiming toward what he termed the "Geist," which can be understood as a mind or spirit, with zeitgeist as a sort of cultural spirit or a cultural consciousness. Marx instead had a materialist conception of history. Rather than the perfection of a societal spirit, he viewed utopia in purely economic terms. Marx did not argue for materialism; he believed it to be obvious. This belief reinforced his total rejection of moral truth and the concept of intrinsic evil.

In industrialized mid-nineteenth-century Europe, the nobility and the aristocracy were very much in charge. Marx and the other young Hegelians understood economics as the primary motivator for all human action and the history of human activity being one of the power and domination of class struggle. The ruling class, or bourgeoisie, have control, and the working class, or proletariat, do not, creating internal conflict. Marx saw the fact of economic disparity as proof of human oppression. In the method of dialectic, the

---

[1]   Paraphrased from Robert C. Tucker, *Philosophy and Myth in Karl Marx* (Cambridge: Cambridge University Press, 1961), p. 39.

tension between the ruling class and the working class would inevitably lead to the revolution of the have-nots against the haves. If social injustice is the cause of human suffering, social justice must be the solution. Through class struggle, Marx believed society can be forced into change and eventually arrive at a materialist, economic utopia.

The Opiate of the Masses

While seemingly the less constrained of the two groups, Marx held that the ruling class is also dependent on the proletariat. The ruling class needs the working class to produce goods as well as to buy what the rulers have to sell. The exploited class should therefore have enough means to afford small comforts and diversions. This helps maintain the economic status quo for the ruling class and allows the underclass to have just enough to turn their gaze away from their misery, placating any felt need for a proletariat revolution.

Beyond the ability to afford some small comforts, Marx believed that the most effective way to distract and appease the working class is religion—what he famously termed the opiate of the people. The underclass is drawn to religion because it eases their pain in this life and gives them hope for the next. It encourages the proletariat to accept their circumstances rather than rebel against them. For a devout Christian worker, adversity, rather than something to resist and reject, is a part of God's will. What's more, adversity and suffering can be ennobling and sanctifying. Imbued with such purpose, instead of an obstacle to his happiness, a Christian is prompted to find real meaning and dignity in suffering well his circumstances.

To Marx, all of this works to the advantage of the bourgeoisie. They welcome religion because it keeps the proletariat subdued and in their place. Marxist revolution only germinates in a populace that is resentful, envious, and angry. The proletariat need to hate their lives and the bourgeoisie enough to grow bloodthirsty.

Without God, Marx believed, man would be empowered, free to shape his reality and become his own god "so that he will revolve round himself and therefore round his true sun. Religion is only the illusory sun which revolves round man as long as he does not revolve round himself."[2]

Their Own True Sun

On a personal level, Marx certainly lived as his own sun around whom his life revolved. His poetry was filled with violence, destruction, and demonic delusions of usurping God. In his letters, he wrote of his understanding that as the Roman Empire was brought to its knees by sexual licentiousness, so could ruination be brought to the West through the breakdown of all sexual restraint and the abolition of the family.[3]

He also wrote extensively about abolishing inheritance, as he considered it (along with all private property) to be an unjust manner of privileging some over others. Yet after years of profligacy with his money, he began routinely asking

---

2   Karl Marx, *Critique of Hegel's Philosophy of the Right* (1844).
3   Ralph de Toledano, *Cry Havoc*, p. 35.

for advances on his inheritance, to which his mother obliged him time and again. When once she refused, he left and did not visit her again. His wife and children spent years in abject poverty, his wife begging him to work to support them. Marx, however, viewed himself as too intellectual to work.

While he wrote about the need to foster despair, Marx's family actually lived it. Four of his six children preceded him in death, and his two surviving daughters committed suicide in joint suicide pacts with their husbands, whom Marx despised.

The family was somewhat financially helped by living off the inheritance of a wealthy Prussian communist, Friedrich Engels, with whom Marx would coauthor *The Communist Manifesto* in 1848. Of Engels, Paul Kengor writes, "He was a proponent of promiscuity and, most of all, easy divorce—which communist regimes of the twentieth century implemented with vigor, and with subsequent huge divorce rates that dealt unprecedented blows to families."[4]

Echoing earlier writings of Marx, Engels argued in *The Origin of the Family* that women ought to become liberated from the oppression of their husbands by entering the factories and the workforce. Marx and Engels laid the foundation for "patriarchy" as a pejorative. Housework should become nationalized, they claimed, and children were to be raised not by parents but communally. Besides advancing the power of the state, these changes would lead to more

---

[4]   Paul Kengor, *Takedown* (WND Books, 2015), p. 29.

women being available for sex by removing their need for the support of a husband or the responsibility of child care.

While providing a greater pool of available women was of personal benefit to Engels, it was also a key part of revolutionizing society. The structure of the family threatened and repulsed Communist theory. "The modern individual family is founded on the open or concealed slavery of the wife. . . . Within the family he is the bourgeois and his wife represents the proletariat."[5]

In a sane world, the works and ideas of Karl Marx would have been left as a footnote in the annals of history. Instead they have been more akin to a recurring cancer or a sexually transmitted disease—continually simmering, spreading, flaring up, and fatal if not checked. His *Communist Manifesto* is the most assigned economic reading in US colleges, and it is somewhat fashionable and not at all uncommon to hear progressive activists refer to themselves as Marxists despite the millions of corpses that have resulted from the implementation of his ideas.[6] Even without explicit reference to him, Marxist ideology animates and undergirds its descendants in the woke movement. Next, we will turn to how he was repackaged and rebranded for the West while still retaining the pernicious fundamentals of his ideology—the rotting fruits of which have become impossible to ignore.

---

[5]   Friedrich Engels, *Origins of the Family, Private Property, and the State,* Part II: The Family.

[6]   Tom Bemis, "Karl Marx is the most assigned economist in U.S. college classes," *Market Watch,* January 31, 2016, https://www.marketwatch.com/story/communist-manifesto-among-top-three-books-assigned-in-college-2016-01-27.

3

Coming to America

Marx had believed revolution was inevitable, but in the
aftermath of the First World War, German Marxists
found themselves disappointed when it failed to materialize.
In order to study what had gone wrong, they formed the
Institute for Social Research (which came to be known as
the Frankfurt School). The one bright spot for them was the
Bolshevik revolution in Moscow, and it was with great hope
that the German Marxists looked to learn from Vladimir
Lenin.

In 1902, Lenin had already argued that a Marxist revolution would not happen spontaneously; it would need to be
brought to them from without, through the influence of an
activist class of intellectuals and professionals, soldiers and
criminals raising their consciousness to their oppression and
converting their anger into revolution.

Lenin thrived on stoking the proletariat and had a visceral
lust for violence. In him we see the early stratagem of justifying anarchy, violence, and destruction in service of action,
change, and societal transformation. "Lenin's solution was
to give arms to detachments of workers and students and
let them get on with revolutionary activity regardless of

whether they belonged to the Russian Social-Democratic Labor Party. The detachments should kill spies, blow up police stations, rob banks and confiscate the resources they need for armed insurrection."[1]

Similarly influencing the new direction of the Frankfurt School was the Italian Communist Antonio Gramsci. He contended through his concept of "Cultural Hegemony" that societal power is not just through economic means but also through cultural domination. The ruling class forwards values, morals, and ideas which benefit them. Christianity was considered by Gramsci to be a particularly dangerous delusion that served only to buttress capitalism and the ruling class. The dominance of these ideas and norms relies on their remaining unquestioned. The duty of every person, therefore, was to be an activist pointing out this domination and fighting to subvert it.

Gramsci's work was famously reformulated in 1967 by the German student movement leader Rudi Dutschke. Dutschke coined the phrase "the long march through the institutions" to indicate the necessity to raise revolutionary consciousness by infiltrating the influential institutions in the West. With tentacles rooted and far-reaching, Marxists could radicalize cultural attitudes by convincing people of the oppression of the old values and norms. Eventually, Gramsci maintained, a socialist hegemony would be established, making revolution possible where it once seemed inconceivable.

---

[1]   Robert Service, *Lenin: A Biography* (Cambridge, MA: Belknap Press, 2002), p. 177.

The operatives of the Frankfurt School developed their own strategy of marching through the institutions in three main areas: the family, the academy, and the culture. Fleeing Hitler's Germany, the Frankfurt School moved into Columbia University in 1935, with famed educator and Soviet sympathizer John Dewey facilitating its incorporation. Their missions coincided. A movement toward neo-Freudianism was already popular among much of the faculty at Columbia, and Communist sympathizers were not uncommon, making it a natural and welcome home for the Frankfurters who sought a fusion of the two.

The Family

Western society, according to the Frankfurt School, promoted a culture deeply resistant to revolution due to an internalized authoritarianism. The means of promulgating this authoritarianism was by way of the patriarchal family. Of this, Ralph de Toledano writes, "In their subconscious, the earlier revolutionist harbored the very authority they were subverting, and they could only free themselves of this, according to the Frankfurt School, by tomcatting and neo-psychoanalysis. The next revolution would first have to depose the father and install the mother."[2] The Frankfurt School architects, many of them plagued by disturbing and perverse sexual histories, preached a doctrine of sexual and cultural freedom. This ideological fusion of neo-Freudianism

---

[2]   Ralph de Toledano, *Cry Havoc* (Anthem Books, 2006), pp. 60–61.

and neo-Marxism would go on to shape the future of the Progressive movement.

Instrumental in discerning this new way forward was György Lukacs. Lukacs came from a wealthy Hungarian family but despised his background and bourgeoise state in life. He also detested gender roles, marriage, and family. In his 1922 work *History and Class Consciousness*, he blamed the failure of the revolution to materialize on the psychology of the working class.

Lukacs's lifelong themes were revolution and sex. As commissar of culture in Hungary, he sought to alter the psychology of the working class by controlling the narratives presented to them. He instituted strict mandates on speech: banning any newspapers he deemed to be too bourgeois, censoring libraries, and instituting writers' guilds with strict instructions on what could and could not be written. He sought to free children of parental authority by ending their religious instruction and replacing it with a radical sex education curriculum.

While a controversial figure to some, Lukacs was valued by Willi Münzenberg, the operational head of Communist International. The two of them bonded over their mutual hatred of Western civilization and culture. They believed "Western civilization was made up of many mansions—the morality that derives from the Old and New Testaments, the traditional family, the respect for the past as a guide to the future, the restraint of man's baser instincts, and a socio-political organization which guaranteed freedom without license. Of these obstacles the greatest were God and family."[3]

If authoritarianism was the subconscious obstacle to revolution, the remedy, according to Lukacs, was psychoanalysis and the subversion of the father. Making men lecherous would engender suspicion and distrust in wives and rebellion in children.

Building on this goal was fellow Frankfurter Wilhelm Reich, born to a secular, progressive Jewish family with an abusive and cold father. His mother carried on a long-term affair, hidden from her husband but with full knowledge of her son from the age of four. As a teen, he exposed his mother's affair to his father, the torment of which led his mother to commit suicide. His distraught father would attempt to do the same.

From an early age, Reich was consumed by sexual desire and activity. In childhood, he had sexual encounters with maids and even sexual fixations with animals. As a young man, circa 1922, he became a protégé of Freud and continued his life of debauchery by taking on a broad range of lovers. He was also enamored with the writings of Marx and Engels and became a natural fit for the Frankfurt School. He officially joined the Communist Party in 1928, intent on sparking revolution through the sexual liberation of culture.

Though not the first, Reich was the most passionate about the need to unite socialism with sexual liberation. He was greatly aided by Freudian principles such as the

---

[3]   Ibid, p. 26.

subconsciousness of desire, the lively sexuality of children, the belief that repressed desire does not lose strength but leads to psychic disturbance, and the understanding that morality is always repressive.

Along with the others of the Frankfurt School, Reich believed the family was authoritarian—both mother and father. His 1936 book *The Sexual Revolution* cemented his legacy as the father of the sexual revolution. Reich, and the Frankfurt School more broadly, was adamant that sexual repression was linked to political repression, prompting him to advocate for the personal and political necessity of infidelity and the total liberation of the libido. His influence is particularly evident in his female disciples who promote in feminist theory pornography, lesbianism, and masturbation as tools to free women of the oppression of men.

Like Lukacs, his aim of sexual liberation applied also to children, who Reich believed should be encouraged to pursue sexual exploration at an early age. To this end, of exceptional importance to Reich was mandated pre-pubescent sexual education. While ostensibly for the sake of simply priming them on the facts of life, in reality Reich et al knew that sex education was a powerful trojan horse. Exposition at a young age to the mechanics and even images of sexual activity would encourage them to imitate and engage in such activity sooner than what would otherwise be likely. Away from the confines of parental authority, early sex education would seize and form their imaginations and corrode their consciences.

Marching Through the Academy

The revolutionary mission of the Frankfurt School would also be fought on the grounds of the universities. This plan held a dual benefit. They knew that by corroding the students' faith in the pillars of Western culture, they could undermine the future stability of that culture. Secondly, they knew they would raise less suspicion and could communicate more freely and internationally by being in the academic world than they would've been able to as an explicitly political organization.

The ideology of the Frankfurt School would shape future generations of children not just by destabilizing the family but by revolutionizing the educational system "to which naïve American parents delivered up their children and particularly to the teachers' colleges."[4] Indeed, the training of teachers would prove to be one of the most effective methods of revolution. The effects are pervasive to this day and will be discussed in detail in subsequent chapters.

Critical theory, the hallmark of the Frankfurt School, transformed the understanding of education away from the goal of knowledge and toward the goal of change. Educators became activists, training legions of students to adopt the revolutionary spirit by criticizing all that is. Critical theory became the method and filter through which all things must be seen. Beyond just influencing the academy, it eventually lead to the politicization of every aspect of society from sports to knitting.

---

4   Paul Kengor, *Takedown* (WND Books, 2015), p. 103.

For critical theory to be effective, it must be three things: explanatory, practical, and normative. To be explanatory, it needs to awaken people to oppression through a compelling narrative such as an origin story. Next, it needs to turn them into activists by giving them practical steps to fight their oppression. Thirdly, it should cloak them with righteousness by conveying the moral weight of their cause. This last aim was the trickiest. While the Frankfurt School sought to disabuse people of belief in an objective moral law, still they needed to give them the emotional thrust of a moral imperative. The revolution requires true believers willing to justify any means, even to the point of bloodshed.

Critical theory, far from being an obscure notion limited to the Frankfurt School, has been the pillar of American elite education for decades now. The effectiveness and fervor that has resulted in today's woke culture was exactly the design of the German revolutionaries who came here to instill it.

Marching Through the Culture

The third main avenue of seeding revolution into society was through the culture. In the late 1920s, Max Horkheimer took over directorship of the Frankfurt School and brought on Theodor Adorno and eventually Herbert Marcuse, Erich Fromm, and others.

Adorno and Horkheimer had internalized Freudian theories of regression, sadomasochism, and *schadenfreude*. Adorno believed we are sadomasochistic subjects, always suffering because of the injustices of society to the point where we begin not just to endure our suffering but to enjoy it.

Adorno applied the concept of *schadenfreude* to explain how the oppressed would escape their dismal lives by taking satisfaction in the suffering of others. *Schadenfreude*, in so far as it served to distract us from our suffering, was an obstacle to revolution.

This desire for *schadenfreude* was especially pronounced for Adorno and Horkheimer in the culture of Hollywood, a place where they spent considerable time. Their encounter with Hollywood was the opposite of all they'd known in Europe. The superficiality, the advertising, and the celebrity obsession were repugnant to their sensibilities, but in it, they recognized the power of popular culture to captivate, control, and alter the masses. Thus, they sought to harness that power into a tool for the sake of revolution. All art and media were to be transformed into avenues of change by turning them into vehicles for cultural criticism. Rather than showing beauty, art should be judged by how effectively it reveals misery and injustice. The purpose of art, they declared, should be strictly political and critical.

For the Frankfurters, a movie like *It's a Wonderful Life,* for example, embodied the worst of art. It conveyed a message that the life you live is good and that the way to happiness is through a shift, not in circumstances, but in personal perspective, enabling a new sense of gratitude for the world you inhabit. Such a movie was contradictory to the aims of the neo-Marxists, making its audience satisfied with, rather than aggrieved by, the status quo of their lives.

The Frankfurters knew that to be an effective avenue of change, art need not accurately reflect the reality it critiqued. An exaggerated depiction of the misery of the world was not only acceptable but encouraged in order to foment revolution. Adorno famously believed that it is only in exaggeration that truth is found. Reality must be presented in a way that is extreme and shocking.

While the movie industry did not change overnight, seeds were planted and roots took hold and spread over time in Hollywood. The Progressive influence over the years has been dramatic. It is hard to imagine only a few decades ago a movie like *Chariots of Fire* was green lit and celebrated. A scan of Oscar contenders over the most recent decade quickly reveals the effectiveness of the Frankfurt School strategy coming to fruition. The common theme in countless movies now is seemingly aimed at raising the consciousness of its audience to the zero-sum power dynamic of oppression based on race, gender, sexuality, or identity. Movies like *Moonlight, The Shape of Water, Crash, Call Me By Your Name, Dallas Buyers Club*, and on and on.

To be fair, some movies about oppression have highlighted real injustices. But even if grounded in reality, recounting and repackaging oppression narratives over and over again distorts our perception of that reality. Freezing and amplifying certain injustices effectively cement a narrative in the minds of the audience that this sort of injustice is more pervasive than the data might suggest. Adorno was correct: in exaggerating a problem, we become awakened to it and lose the objectivity to see the proper scope of the problem. This also explains why in current discussions around hot topics, references to data or statistics is often considered bigotry; reality is not the point—the agenda is.

Building the Army

Perhaps the most influential of all of the Frankfurt School figures was Herbert Marcuse. Marcuse was sometimes critical of Reich, believing he made sexual freedom too much of a panacea. Of their differences however, Paul Kengor writes, "The differences were more akin to two friendly Baptist preachers dissenting in their exegetical interpretation of a certain passage of Scripture rather than taking issue with the entirety of the New Testament. For both Marcuse and Reich, the covenant had been established long ago, with the gospel proclaimed through Marx and Engels. The two apostles, like communist Saints Peter and Paul, simply needed to hash out their extensions of the Freudian-Marxist Pentecost. They quibbled over next steps, but they agreed on their messiah."[5]

Whereas Reich sought to foment revolution through sexuality, Marcuse broadened this strategy by seeking to appeal to the bohemian artists and intellectuals who were already discontent with various aspects of traditional American life. He identified them as ripe for activism and to have their consciousness fixated on oppression. Such bohemian leaders—artists, professors—could in turn raise the consciousness of the youth. Marcuse knew that once they were turned onto this emotionally charged narrative, it would spread like a contagion and turn them against their families and country and other aspects of traditional Western civilization.

Marcuse became a highly effective celebrity intellectual for the youth of the 1960s counterculture, and he encouraged and celebrated their radicalization and violence. In addition

---

5   Ibid., p. 119.

to the bohemians and the students (who often ended up becoming virtually indistinguishable), Marcuse also sought to employ other identity groups for the sake of agitation and revolution. He was influential in the Black Power movement, knowing that exploiting the injustices people of color experienced was an effective means of radicalization.

Marcuse was also convinced of the revolutionary potential of a galvanized Women's movement to bring about the destabilization of the West and actively sought to help spread the burgeoning movement. He mentored Angela Davis, helping her build an intellectual architecture for her work as a black feminist. In 1970, Davis was prosecuted for providing guns used in an armed takeover of a courtroom in Marin County, California, in which four people were killed. After a year in jail, she was ultimately acquitted in 1972. Upon her release, she visited Eastern Bloc countries in the 1970s and '80s and was twice the Communist Party's candidate for vice president. She, like many violent activists of the time, went on to incubate future radicals by garnering distinguished positions in academia, including leadership of the Feminist Studies department at UC Santa Cruz.

Writing of Marcuse's influence in 2014, Ronald Aronson says, "The New Left had to create itself. We lacked continuity with an older radical movement, had no theory at hand to clarify our goals and tasks. So Marcuse's presence and contributions were essential." Marcuse, he went on to say, "helped us to overcome our tentativeness and defy the parent-figures ruling our world." Aronson quotes philosopher Andrew

Feenberg, another Marcuse student, "Our protests were not merely personal, but belonged to history with a capital H."[6]

Marcuse was a galvanizing force for the ideology of the Frankfurt School, and much of its legacy is alive because of his enduring influence on the culture. Through what he termed the "Great Refusal," revolutionaries would forward the cause of history by rejecting all that is. Like Gramsci, he knew revolution would not come overnight but would happen slowly over generations.

Marxism Syndrome by Proxy

Critical theory, established by the Frankfurt School, has become a big tent to accommodate postmodernism, neo-Marxism, and neo-Freudianism. The point is to destabilize, fragment, and eradicate hierarchy, history, meaning, and fundamental human identity. We see this in the dissolution of any stable conception of a human being. A person must be nothing in order to be anything.

Professor Carl R. Trueman writes on this point, "All previous metanarratives have, for good or ill, attempted to provide the world with stability, a set of categories by which cultures can operate. They may have offered different, even mutually exclusive, accounts of the world, but offering stability was still the intention." The baton of critical theory became a sledgehammer with the incorporation of Postmodernism espousing a total rejection of grand narratives. "It

---

6   Ronald Aronson, "Marcuse Today," *Boston Review*, November 17, 2014, http://bostonreview.net/books-ideas/ronald-aronson-herbert -marcuse-one-dimensional-man-today.

is the quintessential ideology of the anti-culture, opposed to any and every form of transcendent authority. And that generates all manner of problems, even in the most unlikely of places."[7]

Without a grand narrative, we have only the dominant narrative of our time. In the void left behind by this crisis of meaning, the only thing left is power, and the only response is violence. It was the encounter with such a violence-filled vacuum in Paris in 1968 that lead Sir Roger Scruton to first understand himself to be on the side of the conservatives. In watching students who revered the French postmodernist Michel Foucault bring riot and destruction into the streets, Scruton observed, "The revolutionary spirit, which searches the world for things to hate, has found in Foucault a new literary formula. Look everywhere for power, he tells his readers, and you will find it. Where there is power there is oppression. And where there is oppression there is the right to destroy. In the street below my window was the translation of that message into deeds."[8]

Over the course of decades, the long march through the institutions of culture envisioned by Gramsci and Marcuse and the Frankfurt School has been like a constant IV drip of poison that slowly kills the West. The evidence of the ideology is everywhere. In the "Parenting" section of the

---

[7]   Carl R. Trueman, "Queer Times," *First Things*, May 21, 2020, https://www.firstthings.com/web-exclusives/2020/05/queer-times.

[8]   Roger Scruton, "Why I became a conservative," *The New Criterion*, February 2003, https://newcriterion.com/issues/2003/2/why-i-became-a-conservative.

Washington Post, a feminist writer penned an essay in 2016 accusing her sons of being part of the problem of a misogynistic system. She relayed how, as a single mother who had suffered sexual abuse, she'd made sure to regularly talk to her teens about consent, rape culture, and misogyny. At dinner one evening, as she was telling them about a sexual assault case in the news, one son rolled his eyes and complained that she thinks everything in the world is about rape culture and sexism. In reaction to their dismissal of the conversation, she writes, "I never imagined I would raise boys who would become men like these. Men who deny rape culture, or who turn a blind eye to sexism. Men who tell me I'm being too sensitive or that I don't understand what teenage boys are like."[9]

The article went viral, and soon her sons' peers were approaching them with phones extended to show what their mother had written. The boys even overheard strangers discussing them on a city bus. They expressed to her that they felt embarrassed and angry.

She responded by doubling down and writing a second follow-up piece titled "I'm Done Pretending Men Are Safe (Even My Sons)." In it she describes her sons as strong, compassionate, and good, but that regardless of those virtues, they are not safe. Quiet misogyny is still misogyny, and by virtue of their being born male, she declared her sons to be guilty: "I know I'm not supposed to cast an entire sex with

---

[9]   Jody Allard, "My teen boys are blind to rape culture," *The Washington Post,* September 14, 2016, https://www.washingtonpost.com/news/parenting/wp/2016/09/14/its-not-enough-to-teach-our-teen-sons-about-consent/.

a single paint brush — not all men . . . but if it's impossible for a white person to grow up without adopting racist ideas, simply because of the environment in which they live, how can I expect men not to subconsciously absorb at least some degree of sexism? White people aren't safe, and men aren't safe, no matter how much I'd like to assure myself that these things aren't true."[10]

This shift from sexism based on one's actions to sexism as inherited like original sin falls right in line with the woke terms of engagement. Official racism oracle Robin D'Angelo premised her best-seller *White Fragility* on the idea that it is impossible to really be a good white person and that the only thing we can do is strive to be less white. Foundational to being white is being anti-black; racism comes woven into Caucasian DNA. This ideology has been injected into our society like a poison. It is now repeated so vociferously and stridently that to question its legitimacy increasingly places a person outside the bounds of polite debate.

In the movie *The Sixth Sense,* Haley Joel Osment plays a child who can see dead people. A young girl who had been chronically sick during her short life reaches out to Osment's character from beyond the grave to give him a video tape, instructing him to show her father. At the girl's wake, Osment's character presents the video to the dad, who is shocked to find that it contains footage of his wife intentionally spiking her daughter's meals with some sort of

---

10   Jody Allard, "I'm Done Pretending Men Are Safe (Even My Sons),"
        Role Reboot, July 6, 2017, http://www.rolereboot.org/culture
        -and-politics/details/2017-07-im-done-pretending-men-safe
        -even-sons/index.html.

poison that causes and maintains the sickness that eventually kills her.

Through this scene, many people were introduced to Munchausen syndrome by proxy, a mental disorder whereby a caretaker (most often a mother) invents, exaggerates, and often causes an illness in her child. People with MSBP seem attentive and motivated by care and compassion. They can recite a litany of alleged poor symptoms and demand tests and procedures to "cure" the child. All the while they skirt data and evidence that run afoul of the illness narrative. In reality, though the child thinks she is sick, it is the caretaker, not the child, who really is sick (though the child might truly become sick as a direct result of the actions of the "compassionate" caretaker). The root issue is not the one being treated.

The overlords and instigators injecting woke ideology into our culture are poisoning us. They fabricate certain injustices, and where true injustice exists, they exacerbate it rather than resolve it. Continual conflict interrupts and breaks down the transmission of cultural meaning and tradition. The goal is to keep us ill, infecting the body of citizens until the body turns against itself endlessly. Wokeness, Inc. has been poisoning young people for decades, telling them they're diseased and in need of their saving care. The ideology can only offer a posture of compassion while withholding that to which true compassion must point: a cure.

PART II

Dogmas

4

Group Over Person

A person with one broken leg, forced to wear a cast for an extended period of time, will discover a predictable consequence of his misfortune. The functioning leg, having to do double duty while the other is out of commission, grows strong, while the other languishes. Similarly, the three ruling dogmas of woke ideology form a sort of unholy trinity of three "persons" (or binaries), each with a broken leg.

The first of the three ruling woke dogmas is the primacy of the group over the person; second is an emphasis on will at the expense of reason or nature; and the third is the elevation of human power in rejection of higher authority. Whereas in the City of God each leg works in concert with the other, in the City of Man, one grows muscular and the other becomes flaccid. It is through these three distorted binaries that the ideology seeks to establish man as both victim and god. We will examine each of these, beginning with the first.

What's in a Name?

In her book *Primal Screams*, Mary Eberstadt compellingly posits that the reason we have become so tribally obsessed with oppressed group identities is directly related to the fracturing of the family as a consequence of the sexual revolution. The dramatic changes in the integrity of family life, reflected in an acute increase in fatherlessness, illegitimacy, infidelity, and divorce, are not merely in correlation to the rise in identity politics. Instead, Eberstadt argues, the loss of our primal identity within the family has created generations of people who are wounded, stunted, and in search of what was withheld from them. In losing the family, we have lost our very selves and are left to desperately grasp at any identity on offer to us, contrived or otherwise.

It is not accidental that one of the first acts of family life is the task of naming a new member. The numbers tattooed on the arms of holocaust survivors and the dehumanization conveyed by them are lingering visual horrors of the holocaust. In dystopian stories, such as *Stranger Things*, a character is sometimes "named" with a number to indicate that she is valued as no more than one in a series. The act of naming is an indication of the belonging and identity formation that is natural to family life. It is a whisper of intimacy and irreplaceability—the child is not just anyone, she is particular. Leadership specialist Dale Carnegie writes, "Remember that a person's name is to that person, the sweetest and most important sound in any language."[1] There's good reason for that. Hearing one's name hints to her that she is known, not for the sake of any instrumental value, but in and of herself.

Targeting of the family is intrinsic to the agenda of woke ideology precisely because of the way the family is meant

---

[1]   "Remembering Names," DaleCarnegie.com, https://www.dalecarnegie.com/en/courses-v2/3741, accessed 08/18/20.

to uphold the dignity of the person and serve as a bulwark against political tribalism. A healthy well-formed family is preventative; it provides the belonging and care that prepares one to walk confidently into adulthood. As the family is weakened, the pull toward tribalism grows, feeds, and repeats itself. The effort to destroy the family has left people yearning for it all the more; without the family, we become susceptible to a facsimile of it.

Pope St. John Paul II famously called the family a "school of love" to convey the way in which the intimacy of family life can lead us, with varying degrees of pain and consolation, to repentance and reverence by prompting and encouraging members to look inward. Tribalism prompts members to look outward; membership is not based on love but on grievance.

Defined by Evil

Other than in the context of the family, questions about what it means to be human are traditionally answered by looking to universals, with a reliance on a shared humanity. What is distinctively human is what we share in common and what separates us from the beasts. In contrast, the woke seek to answer such a fundamental question in a way that renders a shared humanity and commonality impossible: by redefining all people into opposition, each person is defined as oppressor or oppressed or some combination of the two. Relationships serve as a source of power struggle rather than a wellspring of connection.

While the orthodox Christian understanding of personal identity is informed by all sorts of attributes and circumstances, at his core, each person, made in the image and likeness of God, is an irreducible subject with an intellect directed toward truth and a will oriented toward the good. Because truth and goodness are transcendentals of God, at the core of our identity, by our very nature, we are defined in relationship to him. In addition to being distinctively human by our capacity to reason, we achieve our purpose, and are most fully ourselves, in relationship with Love himself.

In contrast, for the woke, we are not to understand ourselves in proximity to the goodness of God but in proximity to the evil of society. Whereas membership in a family is personal, membership in the political tribe is abstract. Each person belongs by virtue of being an instantiation of a movement, like a number on an arm. But while sharing in group membership is necessary, it is not sufficient. What is demanded is to share the ideology as well. *It is the ideology, not the individual, which must flourish.*

For example, if oppression is at the core of womanhood (as the woke say), then woman's perfection exists in fighting her oppression and striving for power. A woman who is not a feminist is denying something central to her womanhood. A conservative gay man is not allowed to represent the gay community. A conservative man of color will have his blackness questioned. This is echoed in a recent statement by the main author of the *New York Times'* "1619 Project," Nikole Hannah-Jones. "There is a difference between being politically black and being racially black. I am not defending anyone, but we all know this and should stop pretending that we don't."[2]

Someone who is racially black can be dismissed, ignored, or vilified by the movement if his politics contradict the movement. In lacking the correct political consciousness, such a person is repressing the core of his identity and should not have a platform. While diversity is the stated goal, uniformity and power are the actual goals. You are only important insofar as you further the agenda.

Woke Supremacy

Vladimir Lenin argued that the oppressed cannot of their own accord sufficiently understand the depths of their oppression and, therefore, need an intellectual class continually reminding them to be angry and feel hated.[3] Marcuse understood this and was cunning and gifted at leading and radicalizing youth by selling them on their despair in the 1960s. Saul Alinsky was another influential radical (who also had a great and well-documented impact on Barack Obama and Hillary Clinton), echoing the importance of revealing to the oppressed their misery. In his book *Rules for Radicals*, he speaks to the necessity of "rubbing raw the sores of discontent" in order to galvanize people for radical social

---

[2]   Valerie Richardson, "Architect of NYT's 1619 project draws distinction between 'politically black and racially black,'" *The Washington Times*, May 22, 2020, https://www.washingtontimes.com/news/2020/may/22/nikole-hannah-jones-1619-project-draws-distinction/.

[3]   V. I. Lenin, *Lenin's Selected Works in Three Volumes*, vol. 1, (Progress Publishers, 1975), pp. 119–271.

change. Alinsky knew revolution would not come without a militant and uncompromising commitment to fueling fury and division in the populace.[4]

One powerful way this narrative of outrage and despair is driven home is through the media's gatekeeping practices of determining which news stories make their way into our homes. In some cases, they simply create the narrative for their "news" agenda and then find a way to concretize it. In 2015, with the Religious Freedom Restoration Act under attack for being "anti-gay," a reporter in search of a villain went to a small-town Indiana pizzeria. She posed a question to the Christian owners about their business practices regarding gay people—would they serve them? Would they cater a hypothetical wedding? The owners told her that while they would never deny service to a gay customer, they could not cater a gay wedding as it would be a violation of their deeply held religious convictions. The national news media went wild, and the story grew viral. It did not matter that the small-town owners had not sought this spotlight nor set out to enter this fray. The news framed the narrative as a pizzeria going public as being anti-gay. That the owners then faced death threats, doxing, and national infamy was not incidental; it was essential to convey the message that these prejudiced and hateful people were outside the bounds of civil society. The greater message conveyed was that *anyone* who held their same beliefs were worthy of contempt as well.

---

[4]   "Saul Alinsky Is the Cause of Our Political Divisions," *The Wall Street Journal*, February 26, 2018, https://www.wsj.com/articles/saul-alinsky-is-the-cause-of-our-political-divisions-1519662559.

From PJ Media's Scott Ott: "If I were forced to mark out a story line, it would be this: A nice lady in a small town tries to be helpful and polite to a lovely young reporter from 'the big city'. . . . In other words, Memories Pizza didn't blast out a news release. They didn't contact the media, nor make a stink on Twitter or Facebook. They didn't even post a sign in the window rejecting gay-wedding catering jobs. They merely answered questions from a novice reporter who strolled into their restaurant one day – who was sent on a mission by an irresponsible news organization."[5]

That no one was being hurt by this small pizzeria doesn't matter. Some totem of regressive and oppressive Christianity needed to be offered up to the woke gods demanding the end to the Religious Freedom Restoration Act. A year later, in reflecting on the chaos that had enveloped him, the pizzeria owner, Kevin O'Connor, said simply, "Out of anger, there seems to be no getting along anymore. If your opinion isn't what somebody else's is, then I'm a dirtbag. Just because I don't agree with you doesn't mean I have to hate you."[6]

This effort at narrative driven political demonization happens regularly and can be employed by all sides. But it is an explicit strategy that flows right from the heart of identity politics. When situated within the whole of woke ideology,

[5] Robby Soave, "Was Memories Pizza a Victim of Irresponsible Journalism? Yes," RFRA, April 2, 2015, https://reason.com/2015/04/02/was-memories-pizza-a-victim-of-irrespons/.

[6] "Walkerton pizzeria once at center of national controversy has now closed," *South Bend Tribune*, April 23, 2018, https://www.southbendtribune.com/news/business/walkerton-pizzeria-once-at-center-of-national-controversy-has-now-closed/article_83b23989-40ef-554f-b4ab-d4657cf0a150.html. Access date 08/31/20.

it becomes particularly pernicious. In his book *The Stakes*, author Michael Anton refers to this process of woke narrative dominance as relying on two instruments: a megaphone and a muzzle. The megaphone amplifies the preferred narrative through mass media, agenda-driven fact-checkers, big business, and incessantly repeated talking points. When combined, they work to launder the ideology and baptize it with institutional gravitas. The muzzle serves to suppress alternative narratives through de-platforming, cancelling, demonizing, and rampant big tech censorship. Within the woke climate—which rejects critical thinking in favor of critical theory—an emotionally driven narrative becomes all-powerful and unassailable.

Woke Fragility

In their book *The Rise of Victimhood Culture*, sociologists Bradley Campbell and Jason Manning examine how different societies establish a cultural code of what values they prioritize and revere, particularly in the area of conflict response. Some cultures have had what can be called an honor culture. In order to resolve a dispute, such honor cultures, like the Wild West, would have something akin to a duel. In an honor culture, reputation is highly valued and people are loathe to appear cowardly or appeal to third parties to resolve their disputes.

In many societies, including in the United States, an honor culture gave way to a dignity culture. In a dignity culture, the general recognition of the inherent worth of each person is prioritized. Insults, in such cultures, are better endured than fought. A person's worth is understood to be objective and independent of another's opinion, unlike in an honor culture, which treats offenses as true harms to personal dignity. Dignity culture tends to be law-based, so appeals to third parties to resolve conflict are normal. The dignity of the person, part of the essential social teaching of the Catholic Church, seems basic to us now because it is the culture in which we find ourselves, but it would have been a radical concept at varying times and places, such as in the brutality and paganism of ancient Rome or in the dehumanization of so many Communist regimes.

The authors argue that dignity culture has been giving way to, and is on a collision course with, the rise of victimhood culture (or social justice culture), which holds identifying and battling oppression as its highest virtue. Unlike in an honor culture, victim status in a victimhood culture bestows moral status on a person; this gives people a positive incentive to take offence and to broadcast that offence. It is similar to dignity culture in that people are willing to appeal to third parties to resolve conflicts, but in a dignity culture, people are far less likely to take offense from small slights ("microaggressions"). Honor cultures share commonality with victimhood cultures in that they take offenses seriously, but in an honor culture, it would be considered shameful to advertise one's victim status, and it is unlikely they would appeal to third parties in settling disputes.[7]

---

[7] Bradley Campbell and Jason Manning, "Microaggression and Moral Cultures," *Comparative Sociology*, vol. 13, no. 6, January 30, 2014, http://booksandjournals.brillonline.com/content/journals/10.1163/15691330-12341332.

There is an internal logic to each culture based on what it values, but it can be challenging to understand the value system without being immersed in it or seeing its premises. Social psychologist Jonathan Haidt comments, "The key idea is that the new moral culture of victimhood fosters 'moral dependence' and an atrophying of the ability to handle small interpersonal matters on one's own. At the same time that it weakens individuals, it creates a society of constant and intense moral conflict as people compete for status as victims or as defenders of victims."[8]

Some of the division and confusion we have been witnessing and feeling stem from this collision of two cultures—one which is primed to feel harmed and hurt and believes it to be their moral right and duty to identify and publicize their wounds, and an older culture which values a thicker skin and does not seek affirmation through the exposure of wounds, and is confounded or cynical when others do.

Oppression Olympics

The engine of the Frankfurt School, critical theory, took on a life of its own as it concerned different categories of oppression. The ideology as applied to racial grievances is termed critical race theory. In 1989, race scholar Kimberlé Crenshaw introduced the concept of intersectionality into critical race theory. Crenshaw believed the existing categories of oppression were oversimplified and inadequate. Her

---

[8]   Jonathan Haidt, "Where microaggressions really come from: A sociological account," *The Righteous Mind* (blog), September 7, 2015, https://righteousmind.com/where-microaggressions-really -come-from/.

contention was that within one person, there could exist multiple oppressed identities, or even a duality of privilege and oppression. So, while black women and white women might both be oppressed as women, black women have a further layer of oppression due to race, whereas white women carry a layer of privilege in their status as racial oppressor. For example, an employer might fulfill expected norms of diversity by hiring a white woman and a black man. While it seems he has met standards in two oppressed categories (women and people of color), the person lost in the intersection is the black woman. Similarly, black men are oppressed based on race but are oppressors based on gender. Mayor Pete Buttegieg, one of the leading candidates in the 2020 Democratic presidential primiaries, being a white male, is an oppressor, but as a gay man, he is also a victim. This concept of intersectionality provided a framework for naming the crossroads at which various forms of oppression can affect a person. Without intersectionality, such compounding of oppression would remain invisible, Crenshaw claimed.[9]

According to the theory, oppression in one category does not cancel out privilege in another. The goal of practicing intersectionality is to be constantly analyzing how oppression or dominance presents itself in one's varying layers of identity. An oppressor's dominance could be compounded by belonging to multiple dominant group identities. Likewise, a person's victim status gains moral stature with the

---

[9]   Kimberlé Crenshaw, "Mapping the Margins: Intersectionality, Identity Politics, and Violence against Women of Color," *Stanford Law Review*, Vol. 43, No. 6 (Jul., 1991).

compounding of her grievances through membership in multiple oppressed groups.

Intersectionality is closely related to standpoint positionality, which is the woke theory that the dominant person cannot see the oppressed perspective, but the oppressed person can see both the dominant and oppressed perspectives. This is because the dominant position is the norm to which all are privy, while the oppressed perspective is invisible to the privileged. For example, a white man can only see reality from a white male perspective. Whereas a white woman can see the man's dominant perspective and the woman's perspective. The more oppressed someone is, the wider her perspective on the world, and consequently, she has more of a right to be heard. Knowledge and truth in this framework are a function of identity. With positionality, an inverse hierarchy is established. Perspective is proof.

Popular clinical psychologist and author Jordan Peterson points to the contrived oversimplification of reducing persons in a way that acknowledges some categories of identity while ignoring others. In thinking through the various possible identifying groups that might adhere in any given person, we can start with race and gender, but how many races and genders must we consider? "Assume (and this is what the modern science suggests) that there are five major human subpopulations: African, European/Middle Eastern, East Asian, inhabitants of Oceania, and denizens of the New World," Peterson states. "Let's assume two sexes and three genders—although many of those concerned with diversity would insist that there are a much larger number of the latter. So that's 5 x 2 x 3 = 30." He then goes on to account for disabilities, citing 20 percent of undergraduates in 2016 who reported a disability in nine different categories from vision impairment to learning and mental disorders. Assuming two divisions (presence / absence) within each of the nine categories, this takes the equation to 30 x 2 x 2 x 2 x 2 x 2 x 2 x 2 x 2 x 2 = 15,360.

Peterson goes on to say that we should include class and economic origin, considering 12 percent of Americans live beneath the poverty line. "If we are truly serious about diversity, and are willing to attribute it to group identity, and are going to apply its dictates to hiring, placement and promotion for every position, then we already have a minimum of 30,000 different categories to consider."

Additionally, Peterson asks why would we not also consider height, strength, attractiveness? In the race to success, each of those categories can play a role. Or what about education, native language, age, marital status, number of dependent children? And there are numerous other categories that can be important contributors in the starting place to success.

Given all of these other categories, "the total of 'diverse' individuals now reaches more than 15 million. We'd only need to add one more binary category—obese/non-obese?— to dramatically exceed the entire 18 million person Canadian workforce." Peterson asks why shouldn't we consider all of those other categories. "Who's to say, given that elimination of discrimination is hypothetically the goal, that one is more important than another? I say this in all seriousness: Isn't that just another form of discrimination?"[10]

While not perfect, true justice demands that each individual be treated as just that: an individual. This is not because circumstances, attributes, advantages, or group identities are not important identifiers that contribute to who we are but because we cannot possibly account for the many and varied nuances that might mitigate or exacerbate one person's handicaps (real or perceived). For instance, should a candidate of color from a wealthy home and good family be privileged in the hiring process over a white candidate who grew up in poverty in an at-risk, abusive home? By focusing only on the approved categories of identity, are we not denying the depth of impact of the other categories? An ideology built on reminding, reemphasizing, compounding, and comparing a woefully incomplete list of grievances ends up being a broad and perverse form of injustice in the name of justice resolution.

Empowering the Oppressed by Weakening Them

The injustice underlying these social justice movements is growing increasingly apparent. An article in left-leaning *Vox* seemed to say as much, noting that "on key measures of racial attitudes, white liberals' opinion has moved to the left of where black and Latino opinions are. White liberals are

10   Jordan Peterson, "Jordan Peterson: Why the Western emphasis on individuals is the ultimate in intersectionality," *National Post*, November 22, 2019, https://nationalpost.com/opinion/jordan-peterson-why-the-western-emphasis-on-individuals-is-the-ultimate-in-intersectionality.

now *less likely* than African Americans to say that black people should be able to get ahead without any special help."[11]

Woke ideology has convinced white progressives to view people of color more dismally than they see themselves, as well as see them as less capable than white people. Identity politics has long been accused of leading to reverse racism, but it turns out it ends in direct racism as well. The Smithsonian National Museum of African American History and Culture featured a chart that claimed to define the characteristics of "whiteness." Among the characteristics listed: objective reasoning, politeness, hard work, reliance on the Scientific Method. The point was to critique the dominance of white culture. The implication of this progressive chart was that people of color are more prone than whites to be lazy, unreasonable, impolite. After the chart went viral in 2020, the Smithsonian removed it from the site.

It is certainly true that some people have advantages in life that others do not. It is also true that there are groups of people who have been deeply and unjustly subjugated by law and by social conventions. For many black Americans, it is an acute reality that persists to this day. But it is a problem that is exacerbated and exploited by an ideology that is built on filtering all of reality through the lens of oppression and, ultimately, in the blatant racism inherent in the effort to categorize groups of people as oppressed.

In an interview in 2015, then president Barack Obama stated that while we have made strides in racism, "slavery,

---

11   Matthew Yglesias, "The Great Awokening," *Vox*, April 1, 2019, https://www.vox.com/2019/3/22/18259865/great-awokening -white-liberals-race-polling-trump-2020, emphasis added.

Jim Crow, discrimination in almost every institution of our lives — you know, that casts a long shadow. And that's still part of our DNA that's passed on."[12] It is an interesting choice of metaphor; DNA is essential, of our very core, permeating throughout each person. This increasingly influential view, called racial essentialism, holds that we must prioritize race over everything else. Some black writers have taken to rebuking racial essentialism, noting the obvious problem that it reduces persons down to their immutable characteristics, which is indistinguishable in principle from the white racism of old that held skin color to be preeminent in the valuation of a human being.[13]

It would not be hard to construct a game of "Who said it? The Racist or the Woke?" Both agree racial identity is of principal importance in categorizing and dividing persons. Both make broad sweeping statements that imply that racial identity is a reliable predictor of behavior. Both want to roll back discrimination laws so race can be taken into account for hiring. Both see whiteness as a privilege. Both believe people of color to be less capable, less reasonable, and less civil than white people.

The ideas in the Smithsonian chart were not unique to its authors. A journalist for the *New York Times* spent many days attending race training seminars. One trainer, Marcus

---

[12]   Bill Chappell, "'We Are Not Cured': Obama Discusses Racism in America With Marc Maron," *NPR*, June 22, 2015, https://www. npr.org/sections/thetwo-way/2015/06/22/416476377/we-are -not-cured-obama-discusses-racism-in-america-with-marc-maron.

[13]   Batya Ungar-Sargon, "A new intelligentsia is pushing back against wokeness," *Forward*, July 22, 2020, https://forward.com/opinion/ 451099/a-new-intelligentsia-is-pushing-back-against-wokeness/.

Moore, taught the group that concepts such as "work before play," "plan for the future," and "adherence to rigid time schedules" were examples of white norms. Moore taught that white culture is obsessed with clock time, punishing students for lateness. He claimed this is but one example of how whiteness undercuts black kids. "The problems come when we say this way of being is the way to be." In school and on into the working world, he lectured, tremendous harm is done by the pervasive rule that black children and adults must "bend to whiteness, in substance, style and format."[14] Whiteness, for the woke, is defined by hard work, planning, and time management. Abilities that they no longer see as realistic for blacks.

The same piece describes an executive with New York City's Department of Education, Leslie Chislett, who has gone through ten mandatory antiracism workshops and is prepared to push back. Chislett has devoted much of her career in education efforts to get more students of color into A.P. classes, most recently through a program called A.P. for All. Of the antiracism workshops, she says, "It's absurd. The city has tens of millions invested in A.P. for All, so my team can give kids access to A.P. classes and help them prepare for A.P. exams that will help them get college degrees, and we're all supposed to think that writing and data are white values? How do all these people not see how inconsistent this is?"[15]

---

14   Daniel Bergner, "'White Fragility' Is Everywhere. But Does Anti-
        racism Training Work?" *The New York Times Magazine*, July 17, 2020,
        https://www.nytimes.com/2020/07/15/magazine/white-fragility
        -robin-diangelo.html.
15   Ibid.

This habit of reintroducing the very injustice that social justice ostensibly seeks to quell is evident in other categories of oppression as well. Women who have fought presumably to be seen as more than sex objects now celebrate Beyonce shaking her barely covered assets in front of a sign emblazoned with the word *Feminist*. It seems the entire career of Jennifer Lopez and other pop stars exist to serve as sex objects while "usefully idiotic" parents (to paraphrase Lenin) pay exorbitant prices to bring pre-pubescent girls to their concerts. To question the wisdom of all of this is to contradict the sex-positivity of the new progressive feminism. All the while, we are teaching girls that their empowerment looks a lot like their objectification.

This all would seem too bizarre and utterly confounding were we ignorant of the history and goals of systemic Marxism. But as every radical knows, the revolution is not born from a stable society of whole persons. It comes from a divided society that is populated by a wounded citizenry who see revolution as their righteous solution. Indeed, to many, it begins to seem like their only option left. Reducing and absorbing the person into an ideological tribe (the first distorted dogma of the woke) might be sufficient to destabilize society, but there is more than one way to skin a cat. Two more, to be precise.

5

Will Over Reason

In the fall of 2018, campus division was fomenting at Azusa Pacific University, an Evangelical Christian university, over a ban on same-sex relationships among faculty and students. At a protest, students wore slogans and carried signs saying "You can be queer and Christian" and "God is non-binary," among other things. At an emotionally charged gathering, one student leading the group addressed the Almighty directly, proclaiming, "This isn't something sinful, God. . . . This is something beautiful. I pray that we continue to live out the mission of being difference-makers, God, that this world be a place of equality, God."[1]

It is difficult to imagine a more insipid Christian witness than a college student addressing the omniscient, all-loving Almighty, who laid the foundations of the earth, informing him what the real deal is now with gay sex. Rather than conforming ourselves to him, we have made ourselves into our own gods around whom God must adjust. Instead of progress, this is the worst form of cultural regression. It is as

Alejandra Reyes-Velarde, "Ban on same-sex couples roils small Christian college: 'This isn't something sinful, God,'" *Los Angeles Times*, October 5, 2018, https://www.latimes.com/local/lanow/la-me -ln-azusa-pacific-university-lgbtq-ban-20181005-story.html.

if the scientific community returned to the pre-Copernican thinking of the sun revolving around the earth.

In order to disobey God, we must first diminish him. We will not adore a being who is our subordinate. We don't stand in awe of what is beneath us. Once diminished, devotion to him becomes not only unnecessary but unreasonable. This is why for so many today, the Christian faith seems to be a sign of weakness, or even stupidity.

In ensuring God revolves around us, we conceive of him as being what he is not, and in that void, we make gods of ourselves. This is at the heart of the will's triumph over reason, over nature, and over God. What we desire becomes right by the sheer fact of our desiring it. It is now we, not he, who know all, love all, are all-powerful. If we keep God around at all, it is for the sake of sentimentalism or custom. Either way, it will not last.

Therapeutic Culture

It is a hallmark of how deeply we have internalized this message that we are regularly taught as wisdom the advice from the disreputable Polonius in *Hamlet*, "To thine own self be true." The modern transformation of ourselves into our own suns is rooted in Freudian psychoanalysis and is expressed in post-1960s therapeutic culture. According to author Darel E. Paul, the goal of psychoanalytic theory has been what he calls the "salvation of the suffering self" through the discovery of unacknowledged sources of psychic suffering. According to Paul, sexual desire plays a particularly prominent role in therapeutic narratives.

"For Freud, sexual drive was the engine of the personality. He believed both men and women are bisexual in nature and direct their sexual drives toward diverse objects. In this way, the therapeutic not only obscures gender differences and grants wide berth to atypical sexual expressions, it also blurs the distinction between normality and pathology, making every self a neurotic one on an eternal quest for 'mental health.'"[2]

Paul goes on to explain that the central therapeutic values are individuality, authenticity, and liberation. Of the first, he writes, "Individual rights, of course, have long been the beating heart of the American creed. Yet the therapeutic turns traditional American individualism into individuality, wedding the former to a romantic sensibility of the self as a unique and creative spirit whose reason for existence is its own expression."[3]

For a personalism based on therapeutic values, our reason for existence is expression: to acknowledge, reveal, and live out our authentic selves based on our personal desires, especially our sexual desires. The concept that there is a moral order to the universe must be rejected if personal flourishing depends on the revelation and expression of a core identity that is identical with our personal predilections. Societal taboos that limit our true selves are an irrational means of repression in this framework.

---

[2]   Darel E. Paul, "Under the Rainbow Banner," *First Things*, June 2020, https://www.firstthings.com/article/2020/06/under-the-rainbow-banner.

[3]   Ibid.

The more unconventional the sexual desire, the more potential a person has for fully living out the therapeutic values of individuality, authenticity, and liberation. The therapeutic value of authenticity, which requires full and unashamed transparency of the sexual self, carries greater value with more unorthodox desires. Such desires require greater defiance of social norms and so give rise to greater liberation in the expression of the inner self.

Queer culture is a most effective apostle of this transformation—from repression to liberation—for just this reason. This explains the popularity of phrases such as "Fly your freak flag" and why pride parades tend to be a competition of the most bizarre and outlandish presentation of self.

Freudian thought married well with identity politics. The connective tissue between the two is that oppression (internal or external) and liberation are the definition and purpose of the person. Giving in to self is not only a human right but a virtue.

It does not take long to realize that a mode of societal behavior founded in disparate passions will inevitably lead to rampant injustices. In this framework, there is no objective limiting principle to rule us, just the raw raging will. All we have left to withstand the inevitable violent collision of competing wills are corporate sermons on consent and an emasculated legal system unmoored from nature.

The Pleasure Principle

The therapeutic self is a radical departure from our traditional concept of human flourishing. The canon of Western thought, being rooted in ancient Greco-Roman philosophy, holds that virtue exists in establishing a harmony between reason and will—that reason must direct the will and elevate man from a pleasure seeker to a rational animal. Through habits of virtue, man can begin to delight in the good itself as the war within himself fades and a true freedom of self-mastery is attained. In this life, self-mastery will never be maintained with perfection; sin is always crouching at the door. Yet as anyone who has disciplined himself day after day in order to run a marathon realizes, what is painful and seemingly impossible at the outset becomes more attainable and rewarding as it takes shape.

For the woke, this pursuit of moral virtue is not only naïve but harmful. Rooted in the Freudian concept of "polymorphous perversity," humans naturally know no taboo against pleasure and seek gratification anywhere and everywhere until we are taught (coerced) in childhood to unnaturally sublimate libido and desire in compliance with societal strictures. The denial of our pleasure is by definition a type of repression that puts us on the path of pursuing what Marcuse called the performance principle or the reality principle. According to Marcuse, any choice for the sake of some perceived good that is out of alignment with our experienced desire is a performative sign of our internal repression. Echoing Freud, Marcuse believed this denial of ourselves for the sake of performance is a traumatic transition out of the freedom of childlike pleasure pursuits into the repression of social conformity—where a person becomes bifurcated into conscious and subconscious desire. True freedom, for Marcuse, required a return to the value system that reignited our desires, especially sexual desire, and liberated us to pursue them, freed from taboo, social mores, and shame.[4]

It is certainly true that a person can get caught up in a performative sort of pursuit of goodness rather than an embodied one. Goodness is an affectation until it is an embodiment. The smoker who quits cold turkey avoids smoking with a clenched jaw and white knuckles. He is not delighting in his newfound discipline. But eventually, the jaw loosens and the thing that seemed irresistible begins to look repulsive. Of course, the struggle is never entirely over. Though a vice's power over us may wane as we grow in virtue, still we must often struggle to swim up-current from our selfishness.

To Marcuse and the new Progressives (echoed in Nadia Bolz-Weber's progressive Christianity), resisting our desires leads to a performative, inauthentic society. Such a society is damaging to the freedom of the person, for it holds that there is a law higher than the law of desire written on the heart of the human person. This higher law, natural law, must be denied in order to liberate man so that he may follow the dictates of his passions.

Rejecting Natural Law

One of the most destructive aims of the woke movement is a wholesale rejection of an enduring nature of the human person and the conception of law based on reason, commonly called natural law. Natural law holds that all things have a form and a telos—a purpose in which lies their

---

4   Herbert Marcuse, *Eros and Civilisation* (Beacon Press), pp. 11–13.

perfection—and that the faculty of reason can analyze the world, discern the natures and purposes of things, and arrive at normative truths based on that knowledge and understanding. In coming to understand what a thing is and what it is for, we can understand how we ought to treat it. The eye is for seeing, the ear for hearing, the lungs are for the sake of breathing. We understand the health of each in light of its function: How well does the eye see? How well does the ear hear? This extends to the human person. There is an enduring human nature, and we can, as rational beings, come to know moral truths by knowing what a person is.

Natural law is not a mere set of rules; rather, it is an understanding that there is an intelligibility to the world, as well as an enduring nature within and around us. It is to look at what we are, body and soul, and to act in harmony with our nature. It serves as a rational guide to individual behavior as well as a standard for the laws which guide society.

It is this telos that serves as a measure for the health of a thing, but also for our personal conduct, as well as a measure to determine if a human law is just or unjust. Martin Luther King Jr. addressed this to great effect when he wrote his "Letter from a Birmingham Jail":

> One may well ask: "How can you advocate breaking some laws and obeying others?" The answer lies in the fact that there are two types of laws: just and unjust. I would be the first to advocate obeying just laws. One has not only a legal but a moral responsibility to obey just laws. Conversely, one has a moral responsibility to

disobey unjust laws. I would agree with St. Augustine
that "an unjust law is no law at all."

Now, what is the difference between the two? How
does one determine whether a law is just or unjust?
A just law is a man-made code that squares with the
moral law or the law of God. An unjust law is a code
that is out of harmony with the moral law. To put it
in the terms of St. Thomas Aquinas: An unjust law
is a human law that is not rooted in eternal law and
natural law.[5]

Another illustration of the applicability and indispensability
of natural law is exemplified in the Nuremberg trials. After
World War II, the Allies established courts in Nuremberg,
Germany to prosecute Nazi officials. The international tri-
bunal rejected any defense reliant upon just having followed
the orders of their superiors. That these officials had been
following the dictates of human law was an insufficient
defense when the conflict between the human law and the
natural law was so stark. Only through an acknowledgment
of the existence of a higher law could the Nazi officials have
been held responsible.

For the woke, natural law is an existential threat, since it
is serves as both an authority and a means of oppression for
the authentic self. The ideologue unwilling to distinguish
between a higher law and a human one dismisses the former
and corrupts the latter. For him, there is not eternal law or

---

5   Martin Luther King Jr., "Letter from a Birmingham Jail," April
     16, 1963, https://www.africa.upenn.edu/Articles_Gen/Letter_
     Birmingham.html.

natural law, there is only desire and human law. A merely human law, severed from natural law, is rooted only in the will of whomever happens to be in power.

In contrast to this vision, when President Abraham Lincoln was asked if he was confident that God was on his side, he famously replied, "Sir, my concern is not whether God is on our side, my greatest concern is to be on God's side, for God is always right."

The very nature of God implies an intelligible moral order to the universe, and denying this order is akin to the denial of gravity. We might be free falling for a time, but at some point, the spiritual physics will cause us to confront the ground.

In the mind of the campus protestor at Azusa Pacific University, it is a Christian act of love to stand for the oppressed person whose same-sex relationship is prohibited on campus. And here is where woke ideology has been effective: so compelling has been the effort to understand good and evil through the filter of group oppression that we no longer see it as possible to claim an objective moral law. The moral law itself is a rebuke to the identarian, so it must be denied.

In his foreword to a 2018 book by transgender activist Sarah McBride, Joe Biden echoed the ideal of the therapeutic self, writing in the foreword, "We are at an inflection point in the fight for transgender equality, what I have called the civil rights issue of our time. And it's not just a singular issue of identity, it's about freeing the soul of America from

the constraints of bigotry, hate, and fear, and opening people's hearts and minds to what binds us all together."[6]

The effect of this maneuver to a seemingly softer and
more compassionate society is not without great peril. Natural law, once rejected, is replaced with sentimentality and
pragmatism. Any evil course of action then can be justified
if it can be said to be for the sake of a good end. This is a
moral consequentialism that is rife with danger. Once we
decide that evil can be done for the sake of some good, we
effectively deny the reality of intrinsic evil and undermine
the intellectual architecture of our moral system.

Bishop Robert Barron speaks to the inevitable violence
that comes with an abandonment of belief in intrinsic evil.
"A very instructive example of the principle is the Terror that
followed the French Revolution," he writes. "Since there had
been (undoubtedly) tremendous injustices done to the poor
by the aristocratic class in eighteenth-century France, anyone perceived to be an enemy of the revolution was, without distinction or discrimination, swept to the guillotine. If
innocents died alongside the guilty, so be it—for it served
the building of the new society."[7]

Moral consequentialism has led to the worst atrocities the
world has known, and yet we have been propagandized to
believe that it is orthodox morality that is on the side of hate.

---

[6]   Joe Biden, foreword to *Tomorrow Will be Different: Love, Loss, and
the Fight for Trans Equality*, by Sarah McBride (Three Rivers Press,
2019).

[7]   Robert Barron, "Why we can't do evil even if good may come,"
Angelus, May 6, 2020, https://angelusnews.com/voices/why-we
-cant-do-evil-even-if-good-may-come/.

Mother Teresa would not have passed this test of "love," nor would Mahatma Ghandi or even Barack Obama circa 2012 when he upheld the understanding of marriage as being between one man and one woman. Cowed by this demagoguery, which has picked up speed and belligerence, many Christians have remained silent for fear of being labeled a hater. Christians have traded the medicine of compassion tethered to truth for a poisonous lie in the appearance of a balm.

Alexander Solzhenitsyn said to American students at his speech at Harvard in 1978, "I have spent all my life under a Communist regime and I will tell you that a society without any objective legal scale is a terrible one indeed. But a society with no other scale than the legal one is not quite worthy of man either."[8]

Having lived in, and been imprisoned by, a society that fully embraced the lie that we can abandon the natural law, Solzhenitsyn knew that liberty, empty of moral content, ends not in freedom but in despair and violence.

Changing Human Nature

A month before the death of Mao Zedong, a Chinese spokesman stated, "Our Western friends sometimes say we are trying to change human nature, and from their point of view they are right. . . . In our view there is no such thing

---

[8]   Alexander Solzhenitsyn, "A World Spilt Apart," June 8, 1978, https://www.solzhenitsyncenter.org/a-world-split-apart.

as human nature, only class nature."[9] Their aim was nothing less than to create the new Maoist man.

In the last of his series of articles about his time in China in 1976 and the Maoist vision of the new man, Robert L. Bartley, an editor for the *Wall Street Journal*, wrote that the promise of the new Maoist man was that our fundamental human nature can be eradicated and rebuilt and divested of all greed. The new Maoist workers would have no regard for their payment but would be purely motivated by the collective good. No pride would exist in the new man, nor would the corresponding desire to elevate himself above his state in life or his fellow workers. In fact, in this ideal society, there would be little to distinguish one man from another, so all would march together. "Even in the longest run, of course, there remains the problem of what instruments to substitute for greed and pride. The best, and one that has at some moments in history actually worked, is religious passion," Bartley wrote. "The People's Republic of China, being avowedly Marxist, is of course avowedly anti-religious. But a secular religion was built around Mao, complete with his red book for its bible. The forte of his widow, Chiang Ch'ing, was bending all culture and all entertainment into constant indoctrination in the religion of China and Mao."[10]

Without religion, which seeks to curb greed and pride internally, the new Maoist man had to be controlled externally through force and fear. Replacing God, the party

---

[9]   Robert L. Bartley, "Mao: The Romantic Revolutionary," *The Wall Street Journal*, October 20, 1976, https://www.wsj.com/articles/SB959818512690152154.

[10]   Ibid.

generated a new religion of the state. Bartley noted that the road to the new man was one littered with horrors. "There were deaths—the argument is over how many millions—as the revolution was consummated. . . . It is not surprising that a political revolutionary setting out to elevate man should end by degrading him. It has happened before. Indeed, it has happened every time."[11]

The force of the Maoist movement and the ideological similarity it bears with the woke movement of today is striking. It might seem unbelievable that we could follow such a path, but time and again, history shows us that human beings are capable of previously unimaginable evils, especially if, hungry for meaning, they are given someone to hate, and the conviction of righteousness in their hatred.

Indeed, the connection between the two ideologies is apparent in the way some communists have so seamlessly made themselves at home with Progressives. When Communism fell in Poland, many staunch comrades pivoted easily to become European Progressives. "The false premise animating both ideologies is that human nature can be changed. Progress toward a utopian goal is measured by how many people have taken on this new human nature," writes author Carrie Gress. Once this new nature is assumed by all, Gress explains, then there will be worldwide happiness. "Until then we have to 'break a few eggs.' The only foreseeable solution from their viewpoint is contained in an unwavering adherence to the party. Should ideological faults be exposed (like famine, misery, chaos, etc.) blame is

---

[11]   Ibid.

pinned on the fact that the ideology hasn't been embraced by everyone."[12]

In the United States, this idea that human nature was a sort of putty that we could mold at will was notoriously enshrined by Supreme Court Justice Anthony Kennedy in the 1992 case of Planned Parenthood v. Casey. "At the heart of liberty is the right to define one's own concept of existence, of meaning, of the universe, and of the mystery of human life." Echoing this sentiment, Hillary Rodham Clinton wrote that her goal was to "remold society by redefining what it means to be a human being in the twentieth century."[13]

Interestingly, this radical deconstruction of the human applies only to certain categories of oppression. Nature must be transformed and distinctions eradicated when such a nature and such distinctions carry moral implications central to the very basis of civilization, such as the family. This is why male and female differences are confused and diminished while racial differences are exaggerated and amplified. Writer Michael Liccione notes this orthodox dogma of the woke, pointing out that the concepts of sex and gender must be deconstructed so as to achieve justice for women and queer people, but the concept of race must be reified so as to achieve justice for people of color. "Thus, realities that are unavoidably important in human life must be culturally dissolved, and a reality that is genetically insignificant must be

---

[12]   Carrie Gress, *The Anti-Mary Exposed* (TAN Books, 2019), p. 54.
[13]   Hillary Clinton, *Living History* (Simon and Shuster, 2003), p. 161.

culturally reinforced by means of identity politics. Neither of course will turn out well."[14]

Removing distinctions between men and women eventually turns them into enemies because their biology demands recognition of those distinctions, distinctions which speak to their treatment of one another in crucial ways. Once biological and sexual realities are rendered meaningless, conduct between men and women breaks down and the burden of that breakdown is born far more by women (and children), who are biologically and psychologically more vulnerable than men. There are duties and reverence owed to women specifically because of such vulnerabilities which make them distinct from men. Once men are absolved of those, the grounding of the mutual respect between the sexes is eliminated. He grows boorish; she grows hardened.

In contrast to the sex distinctions between men and women, racial distinctions do not point to any real or necessary distinction in relationship. While deemphasizing the difference between the sexes leads to estrangement, deemphasizing the differences between races tends to lead to friendship.

In both cases, woke ideology seeks the path of estrangement. Emphasizing and keeping racial difference at the forefront of our thoughts, actions, and institutions turns the races against one another. For the division sought by woke ideology, distinctions between the sexes must be denied and distinctions among the races must be exaggerated so that

---

[14]   Michael Liccione, Facebook, June 18, 2020.

enemies might become more entrenched across broader categories of human beings.

Overriding one's nature as man or woman often is met with internal resistance. Male revolutionaries in the 1960s testify to having been ashamed that they were not easily able to overcome their instincts toward heterosexuality. Surely, they thought, it was a result of bourgeois repression that they were disinclined to have sex with other men. In his book *Underground*, former radical Mark Rudd writes of a married couple in the 1960s who opened their home to him and a fellow male radical as a way to support the cause. When the husband left for work one day, both of his guests bedded his wife. In an effort to quiet any lingering guilt over this, they reminded themselves that they were her liberators, freeing her from the desperation of a bourgeoise life. Author Paul Kengor describes that despite her husband being upset upon learning what had transpired, later the wife "muttered some sappy, sad Freudian-Marxist psychobabble to Rudd, claiming she 'liked her new self' and 'felt free of the old oppressed person.' She was free of the bonds of patriarchy."[15] The revolution required not only the rejection of heterosexuality but also of fidelity.

A contemporary manifestation of this attempt to overcome so-called repressive internal conditioning occurs in the shaming of heterosexual men who are unwilling to sleep with transgender "women" upon discovering that they are biologically male. The ideology holds that the trans person, despite having male biology, is truly a woman if he so identifies,

---

[15]   Paul Kengor, *Takedown* (WND Books, 2015), p. 147.

and that anything short of full affirmation of that identity is based on a societal stigma and bigotry. The straight man then who rejects a trans person as a candidate for intimacy based on that biology must be bigoted.[16]

Like Hegel and Marx before them, the woke hold that we are continuously transforming human nature toward an ideal future state, and it is incumbent on each of us to be on the right side of that historical progression. The revolution comes to each individual by remaking him according to the vision of the revolutionaries. In his book *On Conscience*, Pope Emeritus Benedict XVI, then Cardinal Ratzinger, wrote of this shift: "The concept of truth has been virtually given up and replaced with the concept of progress. Progress itself is the truth. But through this seeming exaltation, progress loses its direction and becomes nullified. For if no direction exists, everything can just as well be regress as progress."[17]

Truth, to the Progressive, is not determined by who is right but by who has won. With postmodern mendacity, the therapeutic self elevates the will over reason and over nature. A person has to be nothing in order to be anything.

---

[16] Jonathan Griffin, "India Willoughby: Is it discriminatory to refuse to date a trans woman?" *BBC News*, January 12, 2018, https://www.bbc.com/news/blogs-trending-42652947.

[17] Joseph Ratzinger, *On Conscience: Two Essays (Bioethics and Culture)* (Ignatius Press, 2007).

6

Power Over Authority

In a famous essay, Mao Zedong wrote that men in China were subjected to the domination of three systems of authority: political, familial, and religious. Women, he claimed, in addition to being dominated by those three systems of authority, were also dominated by men through the authority of the husband. "These four authorities—political, family, religious and masculine—are the embodiment of the whole feudal-patriarchal ideology and system, and are the four thick ropes binding the Chinese people, particularly the peasants."[1]

As a display of severing themselves from these binding ropes of authority, Mao wrote of the necessity of the peasants to overthrow the landlords, whom he declared were the backbone of all the other systems of authority. With the political authority of the landlords overturned, Mao claimed, the authority of the family, of religion, and of the husband would begin to totter. As economies faltered, more wives would be required to work, leading to less dependency

---

[1]   Mao Tse-tung, "Report on an Investigation of the Peasant Movement in Hunan" (March 1927), in *Selected Works of Mao Tse-tung*, Vol. I, pp. 44–46.

on the patriarchal structure of the family. As the familial authority eroded, so would the religious authority.

The essay was written to endorse and encourage the inchoate peasant revolt and to add moral legitimacy to the use of violence in order to flatten political hierarchy and economic disparity. The monstrous legacy we look back on today predictably followed the same pattern common to the implementation of Marxist ideology time and again: suppression of information, destruction of cultural history and iconography, compulsory speech, rounding up of dissidents, labor camps, widespread famine, and a death toll of approximately sixty-five million, all on the road to imposing a collectivized political order in the name of equality and justice.

Like a good Marxist, Mao viewed capitalism and private property as the systemic drivers of injustice because they lead to an inequality of outcome. To correct this inequality, he knew he needed an enraged and violent peasantry. The Chinese Communist Party highlighted the class status of villagers with color-coded strips of cloth: white for landlords, yellow for middle peasants, and red for poor peasants. This served to help the populace see one another primarily as a totem of his group identity and identify which individuals deserved retribution for their class background.

Party leaders orchestrated "struggle sessions" in an effort to correct and deter any dissent among the people. Those suspected of harboring old ideas were subjected to public berating and badgering and forced to confess failures of fidelity to the revolution and to the state. They also held "speaking bitterness" campaigns in which poor peasants were encouraged to upbraid those in higher class groups and speak of the ways they had been hurt in the past while the oppressors remained silent. Peasant resentment was stoked by the party into a fierce rage, and their bitterness was spoken with vehemence and sometimes while sobbing and shouting their pain. These campaigns often ended in violence or the ceremonial execution of a landlord.

But as Mao said in his essay, it was the concept of authority itself which was the final target. Churches were emptied, damaged, and sometimes destroyed. Religious vestments and books were burned. Christians were driven from their homes, made to wear dunce-type hats, and forced to live in miserable conditions. Bishops, priests, and nuns were forced into labor camps. A priest was thrown into the fire after fainting from abuse. Sister Zhang Ergu refused to trample a statue of the Blessed Virgin Mary and was beaten to death with sticks.[2]

Modern Day Struggle Sessions

Sweeping through present day America is the fire and rage of a long simmering cultural revolution that has boiled over into months of violence and protests in the streets. Bystanders are accosted by angry mobs demanding they raise a fist in the air in support of Black Lives Matter. Crowds descend on residential neighborhoods in the middle of the night with bullhorns chanting profanity-laced screeds for residents to literally and figuratively "Wake up." Others chant "Death

---

[2]   Sergio Ticozzi, "The persecution of Catholics during the Cultural Revolution," *AsiaNews*, May 17, 2016, http://www.asianews. it/news-en/The-persecution-of-Catholics-during-the-Cultural -Revolution-37513.html.

to America." Like the revolutionaries in Maoist China, their goalposts move swiftly from justice to vengeance to abolition—of the police and ultimately of authority itself. Far from unrelated, the beheading of statues of Jesus and Mary and the vandalizing and burning of churches occurring alongside the protests and riots are essential to the revolution's aims. It will not end with statues because it is not about statues; it is about attacking the ultimate author whose authority they will not reverence.

There is also the more clinical work of revolution through the installation of critical race theory training sessions in schools, corporations, and government agencies. Journalist Chris Rufo has exposed vast amounts of public records documenting the details of sessions that train employees in the doctrines of the woke. At agencies from the Federal Reserve to the Treasury Department, private diversity trainers guide employees to pledge their allyship.

In 2019, white male employees at Sandia Nuclear Lab were sent to a mandatory three-day re-education workshop entitled "White Men's Caucus on Eliminating Racism, Sexism, and Homophobia in Organizations." Over the course of the workshop, they were trained to understand that what they consider positive attributes, such as "striving for success," "hard work," and "can-do" attitudes, are actually rooted in oppressive white male culture and are devastating to women and people of color. In another session, they were told to publicly recite examples of their white male privilege and write letters to their female and non-white coworkers confessing their privilege and pledging their allyship.[3]

At the helm of much of this training is private diversity consultant (and white male) Howard Ross. "Ross, who created the training, is a fixture in what can be called the 'diversity-industrial complex.'"[4] At these workshops, federal employees are instructed to struggle against their presumed internal racism, evidenced by the pigment of their skin. White managers are asked to provide safe spaces for black employees to be "seen in their pain." White employees are told to be silent and to provide unconditional solidarity and to sit in the discomfort of their racism. Ross has billed the federal government over five million dollars in race consulting fees, as well as workshops on power, privilege, and sexual orientation. Perhaps most hair-raising is that the training ends with an exhortation to take the training to their families. As early as the age of three, employees are told, their children internalize dominance narratives and need to begin their critical theory training.[5]

As a 1960s radical once wrote, "The issue is never the issue. The issue is always the revolution."[6] Tyrannical power

3   Christopher F. Rufo, "Nuclear Consequences," (blog), August 12, 2020, https://christopherrufo.com/national-nuclear-laboratory-training-on-white-privilege-and-white-male-culture/.
4   Christopher F. Rufo, "'White Fragility' Comes to Washington," *City Journal*, July 18, 2020, https://www.city-journal.org/white-fragility-comes-to-washington.
5   Ibid.
6   "The Issue in Never the Issue," Ruth Institute, August 11, 2011, http://www.ruthinstitute.org/ruth-speaks-out/the-issue-is-never-the-issue.

can only be facilitated by reeducating the populace into righteous anger for some and silence and docility for others. The architects and agents of the ideology exploit the sympathies and fears of the masses until they demand the suspension of their freedoms and look to the power of the state to make right their circumstances.

Authority and Fatherhood

Authority has become a fraught word, be it parental authority, fatherhood, or the authority of God or religion. Even the reverence due to history and our ancestors is treated by many with a shrug at best or outright contempt, even violence, in some cases. The destruction of statues and iconoclasm that consistently precedes revolutions are not accidental but rather part of the necessary reprogramming that must occur for a new man and a new society to be erected from the ashes.

It is a natural instinct in the face of a real or perceived mountain of injustice to want to burn it all to the ground rather than reshape anything. In the intemperance of anger, we want a hammer, not a chisel. The danger is that the hammer is indiscriminate; it admits of no nuance. In its destruction, it claims innocence and authority with no regard to what will fill those voids.

An ideological regime change is not a rejection of a particular as much as it is a rejection of a whole. In our progressive fever, it is not this old book we destroy but the reverence for old books generally. It is not that saint whose statue and memory is reviled, it is the concept of sanctity in its entirety which is destroyed. Iconoclasm is directed at not only marble and bronze, paper and text, but also the icons of family and religion, most effectively through the role of fatherhood—human and divine.

There are two common versions of societal authority: authority of office and authority of knowledge. When we speak of someone having authority by virtue of his office, we mean that he holds a commission issued by some higher power. When we speak of someone having a teaching authority, we mean that a person has superior knowledge or powers of judgment. In both cases, the power is bestowed and grounded in something higher.

True authority must be distinguished from authoritarianism. The latter is a type of blind submission in principle to authority, an encumbrance on freedom of thought and action. In government, authoritarian leaders often exercise power without regard to existing bodies of law, or higher law, but instead with the caprice of their will. Their ability to be challenged is diminished and often nonexistent.

Authoritarianism is distinct from, and in opposition to, true authority. Still, Theodor Adorno, from the Frankfurt School, sought to conflate the two and pathologize the concept of authority with what he called the F-scale, the *F* standing for fascism. According to the F-scale, a problematic authoritarian personality and a propensity to fascism is evidenced by participation in a traditional family structure or by participation in a religion. Belief in either parental authority or a religious authority reveals internalized oppression, a deep need for therapeutic help, and a fascistic disposition.[7] Most of us are not familiar with Adorno's F-Scale, but we have been trained culturally to "question authority." This can be a good instinct if it is used as a ward against blind acceptance of people or institutions who deserve an approach of healthy skepticism.

There are countless examples of persons abusing their authority. This can challenge our relationship with authority. For many, it is difficult to understand fatherhood as a natural icon of authority when, for decades, fatherhood has been undermined from without and within.

But even with poor personal examples of authority figures, most people sense what ought to have been. For example, beyond the resistance to admit of fatherly authority, most people can at least reason about what good fatherhood ought to be, which can and should be a sign of what authority more generally ought to be. A good father imposes discipline—not for control, but for the sake of freedom—knowing that boundaries come before self-mastery. A good father empowers his children to gain independence and take on responsibility. In contrast, a tyrannical father uses discipline to manipulate and control, keeping his children afraid and overly dependent.

Once, when I was speaking with a strong, loving, and politically progressive grandmother about her interactions with her grandchildren, she noted with bemusement that no matter how much she and Grandpa might be similar in their grandparenting-styles, there was an inevitable authority that

---

[7]   Ibid.

Grandpa seemed to command over the children that she did not. Maybe it was his deeper, more masculine voice, or his commanding height, she mused. But it seemed as inevitable as it was unintentional. This was not something the children were taught but something they intuited, and it hints to a reality of fathers as icons of authority.

Parents have a natural and fitting authority over their children. Their authority is of both types: a reflection of a commission from above and their possession of superior knowledge to impart to their offspring. They have a knowledge not just about the world around them but also about the particular needs of their children. This is knowledge gained from the intimacy of family life that a neighbor down the street does not have. They are bound by the bonds of their relationship to be intimately invested in the good of their offspring. But it is this intimacy and obligation that makes the abuse of the parental role so devastating. But its abuse is a prompt to reform it, not to abolish it.

In his book *The Beginning of Wisdom*, Leon Kass writes, "Until yesterday, Father was a figure of authority to every young boy. To be sure, authority may have been shared with Mother, but Father was the imposing figure. His superior size and strength promised safety; his voice of authority laid down the rules and established reliable order; his patient instruction encouraged growth."[8]

It is with this understanding of fatherhood that Kass analyzes the story of Noah and Ham. Noah, Ham's father,

---

[8]   Leon Kass, *The Beginning of Wisdom* (University of Chicago Press, 2006), p. 199.

having saved civilization from the flood and formed a covenant with God, grows a vineyard and partakes of its riches beyond moderation, becoming drunk and passing out, only to be found by Ham uncovered in his tent. This is symbolic of great degradation, drunkenness having consumed his rational faculties and nakedness having thieved his dignity before his son. He appears as little more than a beast. While Ham's brothers respond to this undignified state by covering him, Ham, in contrast, seems to relish in it, rushing to tell his brothers about their father's shame. Ham has symbolically deposed his father as a source of authority. Of this, Kass writes, "He is overturned precisely by being reduced to mere male-source of seed. Eliminated is the father of authority, as guide, as teacher of law, custom, and way of life. Ham sees and celebrates only the natural and barest fact of sex; he is blind to everything that makes transmission and rearing possible."[9] Ham sees his father in his basest state, stripped of the deeper, more profound meaning of fatherhood to which his biology is meant to point.

Noah acted against the natural foundations of his authority by acting contrary to the dignity of his role and to the charge of superior judgment. Because he looms so large in the reality and imagination of his children, a father can inspire awe and fear. This is a powerful position and a heavy burden, one which is ripe for abuse but also carries the potential for great heroism. This is why cultivating gentlemen is a societal imperative. The truly powerful man is the holy man, and holiness is gentle and strong. We have seen that mere

---

9   Ibid., p. 206.

human authority, in its fallibility, is often insufficient for the transmission of an enduring moral education. At least, it is a very precarious place to hang our hats. At some point, each person is startled to see his father as an ordinary and flawed human. As a deeply symbolic role meant to point the child to the authority and love of God, the revelation of a father's less-than-perfect humanity can be placed into the proper context of a fallen nature shared by all of humanity. Such a context points us to the supreme need for a loving God. Devoid of this context, the revelation of a formerly revered father's failures can be catastrophic. The distrust and cynicism that can follow a father's fall from grace can too easily spread to a distrust and cynicism of *all* authority, and even of law itself.

Kass notes astutely, "Those who would live without law are destined to live under slavery; those who would 'see through' authority become incapable of exercising authority and must live under the rule of others; those who deny covenant are bound to accept the rule of the stronger—that is slavery and tyranny—precisely what the rule of law was first instituted to prevent."[10]

By making fatherhood optional, we neuter its essence and inject chaos into our understanding of law and hierarchy more generally. The revolutionary knows that in targeting fatherhood, he mortally wounds authority in the culture. Like a child deprived of a father, a culture looks to fill that void. The un-fathered, deprived of real authority in their lives, are the first to yield to the control of authoritarianism.

---

[10]   Ibid., p. 211.

Authenticity

There is an etymological connection between authority and authenticity. The word *authentic* is from the Greek *authentikos*, meaning "original, genuine, principal," and from *authentes*, "one acting on one's own authority." God, as the author of all being, is the only one whose authority is not derivative. For the rest of us, if we have genuine authority, it must be rooted in some way from above. In order for a created being to have authority, he must be subject to authority. An author or teacher has gained superior knowledge to which she is subject. A police officer has authority of office and is constricted by law, but he is not the master of it. A human law has authority only insofar as it conforms to a higher law. Parents are the origin of their children but are also children themselves.

The word *authenticity* today is a buzz word that can have different implications. On the one hand, it can be an exhortation to reject a certain destructive type of perfectionism that leads us to stress performative virtue but conceal and let fester hidden vice. In this usage, to be authentic is akin to sincerity; we strive to reveal rather than conceal our imperfections to those to whom we ought: a confessor, a spouse, intimate friends. This is a good and necessary part of spiritual and moral growth.

A more pervasive contemporary understanding of authenticity, which stems primarily from therapeutic culture, means to present what would traditionally be considered a fault or a sin as a badge of honor. This concept of authenticity is for the sake of freeing ourselves from the prison of social taboos that otherwise would force us into a life of hiding and hypocrisy.

This latter sense of authenticity is a corollary of the therapeutic self and is also integrated into the experience of oppression more generally. James Lindsay writes, "A person may be said to have an 'authentic black voice' (particularly, on the issue of racism), but no black person who speaks against Theory or its conclusions would qualify for such an appellation."[11] Instead, such a person would be accused of inauthenticity, false consciousness, and internalized oppression. For the woke, to be authentic is to be aligned with woke critical theory.

To understand the woke use of the word *authenticity*, Lindsay explains, is to understand that "Theory exists to identify, expose, describe, problematize, disrupt, dismantle, and deconstruct [power dynamics.] That's all Theory does, so the idea of authenticity within Theory must somehow proceed from this understanding."[12]

Two very different and revealing understandings emerge from the seemingly benign and distinct uses of the word *authentic*. For the woke, we become authentic by conforming to and broadcasting our proclivities and by conforming our beliefs and advocacy to woke theory. In other words, authenticity is based on the god of self or the god of ideology. For the Christian, one becomes authentic by struggling against sin with sincerity and by conforming our minds and our lives to God. Our authenticity is bound up with

---

[11]   James Lindsay, "Authentic," *New Discourses*, June 25, 2020, https://newdiscourses.com/tftw-authentic/.

[12]   Ibid.

his authority. In growing more like him, we become more authentically ourselves.

Authenticity, properly understood, is bound up not with power but with true authority, as the etymology hints. God is the originating principle of all being. We become more ourselves, more authentic, and gain more authority through this closeness with our Author. In the Commandments, children are told to obey their parents in the Lord. The command to honor father and mother is the first commandment with a promise: "that it may be well with you and that you may live long on the earth" (Eph 6:3).

For its part, the Catholic Catechism rightly emphasizes the responsibility implicit in authority. "This commandment includes and presupposes the duties of parents, instructors, teachers, leaders, magistrates, those who govern, all who exercise authority over others or over a community of persons."[13] Authority must be connected to structures of hierarchy. If it is identical with power, then it becomes absolute in the hands of whoever wields it. Absolute power corrupts absolutely (to paraphrase Lord Acton) because only a perfect being can bear the weight of power without the accountability which comes from deference to a higher authority.

It is a paradox that rooting of human power in the authority of God results in the empowerment of people. It encourages us to understand our true nature as creatures and prompts us to conform our lives not only to our creator but to reason and reality itself. In contrast, the paradox of

---

[13] *Catechism of the Catholic Church* 2199.

ideology is that it seeks to make man limitless by limiting his world to himself.

In a most perverse way, woke theory promises its disciples power by stripping them of it in two ways: first, by denying them a path of moral agency, prompting them to be slaves of their desire; and second, by defining them around an axis of oppression, making the oppressors irredeemable and the oppressed powerless against the systemic forces aligned against them.

Because it is a movement based on destruction, there must always be some further enemy or oppression to uncover, *lest they be exposed as having attained power themselves.* But eventually in the course of revolution, the power dynamics become inverted. In a struggle session, it was the peasants, not the landlords, who had the upper hand.

What will it look like in our day when the woke oppressed have wrested the reins of power from their oppressors? It might look like corporations paying millions of dollars to train employees on how to pledge their allegiance to woke ideology. It might look like department stores and other large corporations erecting elaborate rainbow window displays for pride week or, often now, the entire month of June. It might also look like the US embassy flying the pride flag, announcing our pelvic creed in countries across the globe. It might look like authorities denying church services of more than twelve people while allowing woke protests of thousands to run rampant in the streets during a global pandemic. It might look like 62 percent of Americans too afraid to speak against any of this.[14] How will we know when the woke have become the new oppressors? We might know it when we see it—if we have eyes to see.

---

[14] Emily Ekins, "Emily Ekins' survey, 'Poll: 62% of americans Say They Have Political Views They're Afraid to Share,' is cited on *The Sean Hannity Show*," CATO Institute, September 14, 2020, video, https://www.cato.org/multimedia/media-highlights-radio/emily -ekins-survey-poll-62-americans-say-they-have-political-66?query ID=473883d6c0abe21fad72f6608c538d2f.

7

The Crowd and the Victim

It is no coincidence that the words *woke* and *mob* are so often and easily paired. A mob is the natural habitat for the woke. It exemplifies each of the three distorted binaries considered: it is impersonal, unreasonable, and power-hungry.

The crowd has a pull on every human being. French literary, cultural, and religious theorist René Girard illuminates this human tendency in recounting the denial of Christ by St. Peter. Having promised Christ that he would never deny him, St. Peter finds himself in the midst of an angry mob eager to condemn Christ. A young woman identifies St. Peter as an outsider, a Galilean, and asks if he is a follower of Jesus. So strong is the pull to be within the circle of united voices that Peter denies Christ three times. The cock then crows, startling him out of his hypnotic groupthink trance.

Girard explains mobs and scapegoats by finding a pattern throughout history of human behavior that begins with what he terms *mimesis*. Mimesis is the anthropological observation that human beings imitate each other. This can be beneficial and necessary for human development, as when a toddler learns words and speech by mimicking what she sees and hears. As we grow, we might strive to emulate a parent, an older sibling, or a hero.

We also mimic each other in our desires and in our dislikes. "Man is the creature who does not know what to desire, and he turns to others in order to make up his mind. We desire what others desire because we imitate their desires."[1] We want what we see others wanting, and we see much of this psychology in marketing and consumption. For example, a house that languishes on the real estate market without offers begins to be seen as less desirable to us because we see it as less desirable to others. Conversely, a house perceived to be highly sought-after tends to increase its desirability in our estimation, as well as in the estimation of others, leading to a snowball effect and bidding wars.

According to Girard, this pattern of mimesis inclines humans toward conflict, and we start to see one another as rivals and competitors. This is a two-step process. First, the objects desired create a rivalry, especially over things that can't be shared. This is one way of understanding why the Ten Commandments focus so directly and repeatedly on covetousness. Second, the rivalry moves from the objects of desire to the desiring subjects, even to the point of leaving the objects behind or destroying them: "I'll do anything to keep you from getting this!" The rivalry becomes so consuming that the subjects start to care less about getting the

---

[1]   René Girard, "Generative Scapegoating," in Robert G. Hammerton-Kelly, ed., *Violent Origins: Walter Burkert, René Girard, and Jonathan Z. Smith on Ritual Killing and Cultural Formation*, p. 122.

previously desired thing, or person, so much as keeping it / him / her from the other.

When conflicts arise, we are prone to align ourselves with the perceived stronger side. Faced with the threat of violence, the crowd tends to gather against the same opponent in search of a scapegoat upon whom to project their guilt and direct their need for blame and violence. In joining others against a common enemy, a sense of solidarity is experienced within the group. Gossip is a microcosm of this tendency. We feel a sensation of bonding with the person with whom we gossip at the expense of the person who is targeted. On a broader scale, we see scapegoating made manifest in racism, or political partisanship, or mass genocide.

This ancient and human phenomenon is why mythology and religions are characterized by scapegoats and the ritualistic sacrifices meant to appease the gods. The victim carries a dual significance—it bears guilt, but it can also be sacralized because of the sense of solidarity it creates in the scapegoaters. In killing the scapegoat, the crowd achieves a sense of peace. However, the catharsis of killing or banishing can only bring temporary peace because the underlying mimetic rivalry system hasn't been touched, leaving intact the perpetuation of the violent cycle without true healing.

This is a (fallen) natural process that happens unconsciously. Girard scholar Alex Lessard noted to me in an email discussion, "The injustice of the scapegoating mechanism is revealed economically throughout the Bible. For example, through Job's innocence versus the advice of his wife and 'friends,' and in Jesus's intervention in the stoning of the adulteress. There is a gradual introduction and spread of consciousness of the unjust working of the whole worldly system."

But it is not until the death of Christ, who is perfect innocence and perfect victim, that the injustice of the cycle of scapegoating is truly exposed. Rather than giving satisfaction to the crowd, his innocence is known and affirmed to the point that his disciples give their lives in defense of this truth. Guilt cannot be found in him, so his death prompts us to contend with our own guilt. God identifies with the victim, not the scapegoaters. He requests forgiveness for them, for they know not what they do, and he is the victim who takes on all sin and guilt in order to wash the world clean with his blood. Through his death and resurrection, and by the workings of the Holy Spirit, we are freed from the cycle of sacred violence.

The Victim-Mob

In another counterfeit perversion of Christianity, the woke elevate and glorify not the one true victim, by whose blood we are united, but the woke mob. The scapegoat they target is ultimately the Logos. The Logos is the Greek word for "reason," "word," or "plan." Jesus Christ, in being the Word made flesh, is the communication of the mind of God which orders and gives meaning and form to the world. The Logos stands in opposition to the ruling characteristics of the woke because he is the mind (*reason*) of God communicated through the *person* of Jesus Christ who is the author and *authority* over all.

Increasingly, the woke proclaim themselves not just in defiance of moral law but as victims of it. Moral law, which is a manifestation of the Logos, becomes a perpetrator with the woke mob as its victim. Emily Keglor, in an interview for the leftist Christian periodical *Sojourners*, epitomizes this idea of moral order as oppression: "The church in America continues to perpetrate spiritual and physical violence against queer and trans people. Standing at the intersection of queerness and Christian faith — and speaking with clarity and conviction for full affirmation and celebration — is key to reducing the continued religious trauma that institutional Christianity seeks to wield. That word of liberation is transformative not only for the LGBTQ+ community but for all communities imprisoned by the bonds of cissexism."[2]

In its perversion of Christianity, the woke elevate and glorify not the one true victim, by whose blood we are made innocent, but the gods of the woke mob by whose victimhood we are made guilty. Woke ideology encourages the behavior of the mob but takes the posture of the scapegoat. In order to accept the serpent's promise that "ye shall be as gods," they have to claim victimhood as their own.

But it is a victimhood not for the sake of unity but for the sake of division. It is a long-held understanding in theology that evil is parasitic. It does not have being but rather is a deprivation of being and so can only exist by distorting the good. Its nature is to consume and destroy the good it invades. Evil wants to do this with Christ.

---

[2]   Paola Fuentes Gleghorn, "10 Christian Women Shaping the Church in 2020," *Sojourners*, March 5, 2020, https://sojo.net/articles/10-christian-women-shaping-church-2020.

Though the victim gods can attack Christ and his Church, they cannot defeat him. The innocent victim is the ultimate victor. No matter how powerful they become, the one thing they cannot grasp for themselves is Christ's innocence.

This leads the woke ideologues to prowl after the next best thing: innocence in this world. Innocence in this world is a signpost pointing to Christ, forcing the beholder to examine himself. Understanding this makes some sense of the bizarre way in which woke movements want to consume and destroy innocence. The city of man wants the glory of God for itself.

In their failure to make themselves innocent, they have two strategies to deflect from personal guilt. The first is by maintaining the status of victim in order to emphasize the guilt of the other. Raising the moral status of victimhood increases the incentive to publicize grievances and makes the aggrieved more prone to highlight their victim identity. Of the moral stature assumed by victims today, sociologists Bradley Campbell and Jason Manning state, "Their adversaries are privileged and blameworthy, but they themselves are pitiable and blameless."[3]

The second strategy to deflect from their guilt is by attacking innocence directly, as it stands as an existential judgment of us all. As discussed previously, innocence is not possible if persons are defined by evil. For the woke, it is imperative to disabuse people of the illusion of innocence.

---

[3]   B. Campbell and J. Manning, "Microaggression and moral cultures," *Comparative Sociology*, 13, 2014, pp. 707–8.

Prowling for Innocence

We see this second strategy in the effort to sexualize children at younger and younger ages, and in the corruption and hyper sexualization of women, all in the name of liberation.

Innocence, in the world of critical theory, is dominance. We see this most clearly in children. Their innocence is a threat to woke ideology. Protecting childhood innocence generally means shielding them from adult sexuality, sexual perversions, violence. But shielding them from these things has two ramifications: it allows them to maintain that traditional sexual behavior between one man and one woman in marriage is the norm, and therefore the preferred and dominant way of being. Sexuality that veers from these norms then is said to be marginalized by them. This leads to the second ramification: children being sheltered from perversion discourages children who might be inclined toward such things from acting out on their desires for fear of being shamed or seeming weird.

When the definition of the person is structured around oppression, then everyone must be implicated. Gangs require initiations, especially murderous ones, because complicity is a powerful tool. You are in this tribe now, united in the blood of guilt. Complicity distorts our reason, perverts our objectivity, and leaves us with misplaced, irrational loyalties. Until the gang member is complicit, he is a threat.

In 2019, Catholic writer Sohrab Ahmari put a spotlight on drag queen story hour as a cultural moment which demanded Christians stand up and say "no!" Debates ensued, and some fellow conservative interlocutors tended to focus on free speech laws, missing the deeper point. The brazen-ness of the ideology behind this burgeoning effort in pub-lic libraries was another stake in the ground declaring the new moral goal of society: disrupting the natural instincts of innocent children by training them to undo their gender binaries and reconstruct them to think in terms of gender fluidity. It was not about carving out free speech—it was about revolutionizing thought.

Multiple videos appeared of men dressed as women teach-ing children to turn their backs, bend over, and shake their bottoms.[4] In the videos, woke parents smile and nod to their kids. Some children laugh, others look nervous or uncom-fortable. To the woke, that discomfort is their innate, big-oted instincts which the trans activists are here to reprogram.

The merger of drag queens and library story hours orig-inated in San Francisco in 2015 but have spread across the states and across the pond. The stated effort of drag queen story hour is teaching children to be tolerant. The less stated, but still open, goal is that trans activism in libraries can help a child who might be inclined to some sort of other sexual identity become open to her options. The even less-stated but fundamental goal is, unsurprisingly, to disrupt the oppressive power dominance of heteronormativity and cisnormativity.

It is not just trans activism that is trending; local librar-ies are also helping kids walk the grooming plank. In 2020,

---

4   For those who wish to see some of these clips, you can find them here: https://www.youtube.com/watch?v=jkZujRnHWNA. One should be warned of how disturbing these videos are, but watch-ing them is important, as it shows the perversion of this evil.

a Maryland public library hosted their second lesbian pole dancer's "teens-only" sex ed class for twelve- to seventeen-year-olds—no parents allowed. The host, Bianca Palmisano, is openly into BDSM (bondage, discipline, sadism, masochism) and has also expressed support and a desire to normalize among the youth such things as "polyamorous relationships, homosexuality, prostitution, drug use, swingers, anal sex, etcetera."[5] All the while, woke parents sit outside waiting to hear what twelve-year-old Ashleigh learned about pole dancing and sadism at the library. The slow march through the institution is robustly inclusive of the library system.

Gender Dysphoria

Another highly disturbing way the woke attack innocence is through the incorporation of children into the social contagion of gender dysphoria. In her book *Irreversible Damage: The Transgender Craze Seducing Our Daughters*, Abigail Shrier writes of the heartbreaking explosion of girls transitioning now seemingly out of nowhere. A young girl who, at another time, would have been considered a tomboy is now told she is trans. "Teens and tweens today are everywhere pressed to locate themselves on a gender spectrum and within a sexual taxonomy—long before they have finished the sexual development that would otherwise guide discovery of who they are or what they desire."[6]

---

5   Doug Mainwaring, "Rural public library will again host lesbian pole-dancer's 'teens only' sex ed class," *LifeSite News*, January 6, 2020, https://www.lifesitenews.com/news/rural-public-library-will -again-host-lesbian-pole-dancers-teens-only-sex-ed-class.

6   Abigail Shrier, *Irreversible Damage: The Transgender Craze Seducing*

Shrier came to discover that this is an epidemic that has exploded over the past decade. Historically, trans teens were overwhelmingly boys, but now girls with no childhood history of gender dysphoria discover with their friend groups that they want to be trans and push for surgeries and hormones. Progressive parents tend to be supportive. Parents who express hesitation are regularly declared to be transphobic by their children and their children's friends. In many places, there are laws banning conversion therapy, so therapists are prohibited from helping a child become comfortable in her biological gender, even if the therapist can tell there are other mental or emotional issues that are being masked by the desire to transition.

Shrier discovered that correlating with this rise in young female dysphoria is a mental health crisis that seems to be linked in part to the prevalence of social media and the harsh way it affects girls. Shrier says, "And because of all sorts of things in the culture that have allowed transgender identification to really rise in cultural value, this is one thing that young girls have latched onto as an explanation for what's wrong with them: 'Oh it must be gender dysphoria.'"[7]

In an interview with writer Spencer Klavan, Abilash Gopal, an MD who worked in adolescent psychiatric hospitals, states that almost all the trans kids have behavior problems. "They're trying to get attention, other kids don't like them, they don't feel attractive, they're not successful

Our Daughters (Regnery, 2020).

7   Abigail Shrier, "Abigail Shrier: Transgenderism's 'IRREVERSIBLE DAMAGE,'" on the Dennis Prager Show, YouTube video, June 30, 2020, https://www.youtube.com/watch?v=-23nuQrE_qA.

academically." Gopal continues, "But this gives them the mantle of victimhood. And suddenly, all these resources, all this attention is showered upon them. And they also don't have to grow up. Literally, that's what taking hormone suppressants is."[8] Hormone suppressants block puberty hormones, which is why the transactivist wisdom is to transition prepubescent children rather than wait.

Klavan observes that Gopal is an extreme exception in his field. In both the medical field and in public schools, it is verboten to express any concern about the wisdom of giving hormone suppressants (and later surgery) to prepubescents. Any child who expresses a desire to transition is to be given a gender plan and their parents are only informed if the school has an assurance that they will be supportive. Similarly, in his research, Klavan found that there is an intense code of silence enforced by extreme bullying for any trans person who de-transitions or speaks out against transitioning from experience.[9]

Shrier, in her research, tells of a kindergarten classroom where teachers tell the kids that their sex was randomly decided at birth; consequently, it is now the children's mission to find what their gender actually is and that anyone who might question this process is abusive. "This is all done under the guise of anti-bullying, which means that child's parents cannot opt their children out. It is mandatory. . . . The pretext is that in order to protect children, you need

---

8   Spencer Klavan, "Children and Transgenderism," *The American Mind*, April 16, 2020, https://americanmind.org/essays/children-and-transgenderism/.

9   Ibid.

to indoctrinate the entire student population in gender confusion."[10]

Helping Kids Fly Their Freak Flag

Messages are seeded in multiple ways and through various channels to reorient children and fulfill what the revolutionaries deemed the necessary liberation of the therapeutic self. Children's movies, which once were stories of battles and bravery, true love and defeating evil, now have developed an almost universal theme of daring to embrace your inner unconventionality. While this sort of lesson might have its place, the prevalence and ubiquity of this modern morality tale, like the freeing of the therapeutic self, is for the sake of an agenda of powerful people: to encourage kids to find meaning in tapping into their inner freak—the freakier the better.

In the children's movie *Frozen*, Elsa has a secret that makes her different. Her concerned parents take her to see the wise trolls who declare that she was "born this way." She hides her secret, keeping herself in a metaphorical closet. Characters sing about how "love is an open door," reinforcing the in-the-closet theme. When the more traditional people in the village discover that she is different, they condemn her, confirming to the audience that the true villains in life are the dominant oppressors upholding normativity. Elsa moves

---

[10] Allison Schuster, "Speaker: Most Parents Have No Idea Their Kids' Schools Are Pushing Insane Transgender Ideology," *The Federalist*, July 28, 2020, https://thefederalist.com/2020/07/28/speaker-most-parents-have-no-idea-their-kids-schools-are-pushing-insane-transgender-ideology/.

to the mountains and transforms herself into a fabulous queen of her own universe, and in the triumphant coming-out anthem "Let It Go," she sings about how she no longer has to be the good girl, "No right, no wrong, no rules for me . . . I'm free!"

To give another example, when the movie *Trolls* came out (not to be confused with the wise trolls who counsel Elsa in *Frozen*), one woke writer breathlessly reviewed it to be the "gayest movie ever." "There were trolls covered in glitter and sparkles, reflecting light off them like little disco balls. Don't forget the troll that literally [poops] cupcakes. Or, there's that moment when Poppy and her troll friends turn into a rainbow wig to help a sad Bergen girl. And what song do they decide to sing? The 'I'm Coming Out' song, complete with stellar dance moves, a jumpsuit and high platform shoes. Hello Drag Queens! Dreamworks couldn't have been more subtle if they tried. There was no holding back the rainbows emanating from our theater last night."[11]

This is not fever-pitch culture war paranoid hysteria; it is the work of an unabashed ideology hoping to evangelize and indoctrinate the young into its dogmas and practices. It has been happening for years; they are just no longer as concerned about concealing it.

---

[11]   "Trolls: The gayest movie this year," *writing living breathing* (blog), accessed October 16, 2020, https://writinglivingbreathing.word press.com/2016/11/06/trolls-the-gayest-movie-this-year/.

Grooming Girls

In 2017 (and rebooted in 2019), *Teen Vogue*, a magazine aimed at girls aged twelve to seventeen, came out with a "Guide to Anal Sex" full of tips and encouragement and a message that there is nothing wrong with sodomy (not that they referred to it as that) and in fact it could be a lot of fun. Some cautions were included such as, "If you regularly engage in anal sex, particularly with gay or bisexual men who are not monogamous, you might also consider taking PrEP."[12] PrEP is a drug intended to enable sex with HIV-positive people by making HIV transmission less likely—but still not completely "safe." The article was full of nauseating tips and a warning that fecal matter might be involved. The writer quickly assured the kids not to worry! That is just part of the fun.

This same magazine has also featured an article singing the praises of Karl Marx as a revolutionary who fought for the working class against the oppressive rich and inspired movements in Soviet Russia, China, Cuba, etc. There is no mention of the millions of corpses that resulted from his diabolical ideas, his raging racism, misogyny, and obsession with destruction. Instead, it is capitalism that is claimed to be violent, and the readers are encouraged to understand the revolutionary spirit and discern how they can apply it to today.[13]

---

12   Gigi Engle, "Anal Sex: Safety, How tos, Tips, and More," *Teen Vogue*, November 12, 2019, https://www.teenvogue.com/story/anal-sex-what-you-need-to-know.

13   Adryan Corcione, "Who Is Karl Marx: Meet the Anti-Capitalist Scholar," *Teen Vogue*, May 10, 2018, https://www.teenvogue.com/story/who-is-karl-marx.

Middle school girls are learning from such sources as *Teen Vogue* and putting these lessons into action. An acquaintance of mine was horrified to discover from her daughter that anal sex had become normal, and somewhat expected, at her middle school. There are too many examples of grooming girls: from Planned Parenthood protecting child predators to the entire ethos of the brand Pink, a lingerie shop targeting teens and owned by one of Jeffrey Epstein's former close associates. From *The Atlantic*: "Pink features bright colors, like candy, and includes pajamas, swimwear, skin care, and accessories, as well as underwear. In 2013, Pink launched a marketing campaign called 'Bright Young Things,' which drew attention to lacy underwear emblazoned with I DARE YOU across the rear, beach towels and tote bags that read KISS ME, and a T-shirt with a low neckline that read ENJOY THE VIEW. Most disturbing: a pink-and-orange thong with CALL ME printed on the crotch."[14]

Like so much of marketing to girls, the real audience is bad men. No wonder the trans and androgyny movements holds such sway for teens. For a girl who is inundated with the putrefying rot of the sexual revolution, it might start to look appealing to divest herself of her sexuality altogether.

The evil is difficult to wrap our minds around, but we had better. The architects of the Frankfurt School could not have fathomed how effective their plan would be to attack every aspect of the family, including the youngest members.

---

14   Moira Donegan, "The Jeffrey Epstein-Victoria's Secret Connection," *The Atlantic*, August 6, 2019, https://www.theatlantic.com/ideas/archive/2019/08/victorias-secret-epstein/595507/.

The Sacred Cow

The ultimate attack on innocence in this world is waged on the clearest exemplar of innocence: a baby. It is no coincidence that the most visible icon of women's liberation is a place where innocence goes to die, quite literally. Against the ethos of family stands the preeminent billion-dollar industry of Planned Parenthood, innocuously referred to as a vehicle for "family planning." Its influence permeates every hot-pink-hatted progressive march. It is the place where rupture comes to us most intimately. It is where we go to be severed from our kin, from our biology, from an acknowledgment of our existential need. It is where we go to pretend that sex, the most intimate physical act of knowing, is one that creates no ties and requires no intimacy.

Abortion is the sacrament and greatest symbol of woke religion because in one act, it destroys each icon of the family: the child, the father, and the mother. All three are corrupted and made to become contrary to their nature. Man is able to impregnate woman but obligated to neither the woman nor the "product of conception" (in the sterile vernacular of the abortion industry). Meanwhile, woman is also liberated from any bond to man or to their child inside. In this dystopian vision of humanity, each of us is an island, autonomous and adrift—void of duty and hardened to love. Woman and child, united in one body, walk into Planned Parenthood and emerge dismantled and shattered: one literally, the other symbolically and spiritually. Another tie is severed, and she is deeply and profoundly alone.

With a death toll around fifty-six million per year worldwide, there is hardly anyone who has not been in some
proximity or connection to abortion. Anyone who knows
someone who carries this in her past knows it to be a lifelong struggle of sadness and guilt. Depression and regret
are common. But we are not supposed to talk about that.
The disconnect with the abortion messaging could not be
starker. Women are told to "shout their abortions" with
pride. Abortion is the sacred cow of the new left, and for
good reason. It is like Advil holding back the symptoms of
a tumor. It is a mask, a backstop, a cardboard façade. The
reality is that there is no possible world in which everyone's
will can run rampant without that world becoming violent.
Sermons about consent won't resolve it.

Women, who are called to be icons of innocence, are
particularly targeted as such by the ideology. We see this in
the bizarre trend of women using public nudity to protest
against pro-life laws. It is difficult to make sense of this form
of protest until we realize that the publicly nude woman is
an icon of rebellion, a forsaking of innocence.

When legislators in Utah passed a law to ban all abortions in 2020 (with the exceptions of incest or the life of
the mother), the satanic temple spoke out against the law,
claiming it violated their religious freedom. They saw abortion as a sacred satanic ritual. On their website, they walk
women through how to perform the sacred abortion rituals,
including staring at themselves in the mirror and reciting
their sacred tenets, such as tenet III: "One's body is inviola-
ble, subject to one's own will alone." And reciting their personal affirmation, "By my body, my blood, By my will it is

done."[15] Here again we see the demonic inversion of Christianity, with its diabolical mockery of Christ's generous gift of his sacred body and blood in the sacrament of the Holy Eucharist, not to mention the rebellion against one of the tenets of the Lord's Prayer: not *thy* will, but *my* will be done.

Evil has sought to attack Christ and his holy innocence from the very beginning of his life. While we should meditate on all aspects of Christ's life, his infancy is where he is particularly remembered and celebrated in the cultural imagination. Far from a saccharine sentimental story for Christmas, we should remember that though he enters the world simply, it is still in the shadow of the cross and King Herod's slaughter of the innocents.

Childlike

It is not just the innocence of children but the innocence of all people that woke ideology attacks. Through Christ, we are made anew and called to be spiritual adults, but with the innocence of children. We are to be childlike, though not childish. Our fundamental identity is children of a loving father, with the characteristics that such love implies: trust, a desire to follow, an easy eagerness to be forgiven and a swift sorrow for our transgressions, a confidence in the depth of his love for us, and a natural reverence for him.

The dogmas of the ideology serve to strip us of this fundamental reality of our humanity that speaks to us of our

---

[15] "Satanic Abortions are Protected by Religious Liberty Laws," The Satanic Temple, accessed October 23, 2020, https://announcement .thesatanictemple.com/rrr-campaign41280784.

being children of God: embodied, with a nature, and created. The reduction of the person, the rejection of nature and the elevation of the will, the flattening of authority—all of this contributes to, and happens by way of, the destruction of the family. The plot has been largely successful, but it does not have the last word.

Part III

Indoctrination

8

The Sexual Revolution

In his 1936 book *Sex and Culture*, J. D. Unwin published the results of his extensive research studying eighty-six societies and civilizations to see if there is a relationship between sexual freedom and the flourishing of cultures. Unwin, a social anthropologist from Oxford, measured flourishing in terms of art, architecture, agriculture, engineering, literature, and so forth. He divided his inquiry into multiple categories, including restraint before and after marriage. The single most influential factor in determining the flourishing of a society, Unwin discovered, was whether prenuptial chastity was a strict social norm or not; when this was combined with absolute monogamy, the society flourished all the more.

Of this finding, Unwin scholar Kirk Durston notes, "Rationalist cultures that retained this combination for at least three generations exceeded all other cultures in every area, including literature, art, science, architecture, engineering, and agriculture."[1]

---

[1] Kirk Durstan, "Why Sexual Morality May be Far more Important than You Ever Thought," *Quest* (blog), accessed October 25, 2020, https://www.kirkdurston.com/blog/unwin?rq=sexual%20morality.

Unwin found that if there were a societal change in the norms regarding sexual restraint, either toward more sexual freedom or toward greater sexual restraint, the full effect of the change was not realized until the third generation. Change takes root slowly in the first generation, becomes more normalized in the second, and by the third, realizes its full effect on the society. At that point, when total sexual liberty is embraced, the society "is characterized by people who have little interest in much else other than their own wants and needs. At this level, the culture is usually conquered or taken over by another culture with greater social energy."[2]

Unwin discovered that there is a deep correlation between prenuptial chastity and absolute monogamy, deism, and rational thinking. When the first was abandoned, the remaining disappeared within three generations.

Generations are generally considered to cover a span of twenty to thirty years. Let us say thirty. If we consider the sexual revolution to have begun in the mid-1960s when it erupted (though it was seeded and simmering decades prior), then we are at the end of the second generation and entering the third. According to Unwin's findings, short of a dramatic pivot, we are entering the beginning of societal collapse.

The revolutionaries, from Marx to Marcuse, seemed to know this with remarkable prescience. Their plan to demolish the family, though it sounds like the rantings of a madman, has turned out to be the most obvious and yet insidious tactic in their playbook. Like a long-term game of Jenga,

---

[2]　　Ibid.

pull at one stabilizing piece of the tower and the entire thing collapses in on itself.

Religion and the nuclear family stood as the biggest hurdles in the way of the revolution. How were they to dismantle such a basic human institution that fulfilled fundamental human desires? For a sincere Christian family striving to serve God and one another, family life could prove to be greatly rewarding and happy, albeit simple and unsung. Even if told that they were in an oppressive institution, many would still be content in their roles as loving wives, devoted husbands, or religious, shunning the call to resentment and revolution.

This posed a problem, but one which the architects of revolution in America were prepared to face. Weakening the sexual mores of culture is at the heart of dismantling the family by way of the father initially, though it can, and often does, begin by way of the woman as well. Through sexual coarseness, the father becomes weak and devoid of moral authority, the wife becomes devalued and resentful, and the children grow cynical and rebellious. Everyone becomes wounded.

Convincing people that they are defined by pain and evil is a lot simpler if they know the depths of pain and evil personally. Woundedness is exploited and exacerbated for the sake of making tribal loyalties more militant and resentment more calcified. In making family life painful, we did not eliminate our need for one, we just relocated it. The result is a people not only suspicious of the good but trained to defensively recoil from it, and who subsequently go out in a futile search for a facsimile of it.

The Early Signs of Destruction

The destruction was apparent early on, but there were political reasons to ignore it. In the 1960s, sociologist and future senator Daniel Patrick Moynihan was hard at work developing policy for President Johnson's war on poverty. While analyzing statistics and social patterns, Moynihan noticed that the metrics of success for black communities was diminishing significantly rather than improving in the wake of civil rights successes. Some of this was attributable to lingering racism and the effects of years of injustice. But fundamentally, Moynihan determined the problem was the disintegration of the family and that the nation needed to rally behind a common purpose of saving and supporting the stability of black family life. The trend of black male employment and welfare enrollment had begun to diverge pointedly—the former going down sharply as the latter rose. With declining opportunities for employment and the ability to support their families, Moynihan surmised that men would become alienated from the meaningful role of fatherhood, leading to sharp increases in divorce, out-of-wedlock births, and fatherless communities.

The reality he discovered, as supported by all indices, was that the post-war trend for black urban families was toward disintegration, rendering poverty and pathologies that much more intractable. President Johnson was compelled by the report to give a speech at Howard University, where he declared this issue was "the next and more profound stage of the battle for civil rights." The president went on to ascribe causation as multi-varied and called for greater social aid, realizing that the breakdown of the family would lead to untold damage. Generations of children and communities across the country would be crippled.

Though Johnson viewed this as his greatest civil rights speech, he was attacked in its wake. Civil servants and government bureaucrats muttered about the report's "subtle racism."[3] The message was clear: the system was to be blamed and blamed entirely. To imply that there was any degree of solution to be found in encouraging and maintaining traditional family structures was too bourgeois to tolerate. Writing for the *New York Times* decades later, Nicholas Kristoff said, "Liberals brutally denounced Moynihan as a racist. He himself had grown up in a single-mother household and worked as a shoeshine boy at the corner of Broadway and 43rd Street in Manhattan, yet he was accused of being aloof and patronizing, and of 'blaming the victim.'" Kristoff quotes Floyd McKissick, then a prominent civil rights leader, as saying, "My major criticism of the report is that it assumes that middle-class American values are the correct values for everyone in America."[4]

While the traditional family is written off as a remedy, more sinister solutions to poverty take root. The foundress of Planned Parenthood, Margaret Sanger, was a notorious racist and did not hide the fact that birth control and

[3]   Kay S. Hymnowitz, "The Black Family: 40 Years of Lies," *City Journal*, Summer 2005, https://www.city-journal.org/html/black -family-40-years-lies-12872.html.

[4]   Nicholas Kristof, "When Liberals Blew It," *The New York Times*, March 11, 2015, https://www.nytimes.com/2015/03/12/opinion/ when-liberals-blew-it.html.

abortion were essential to eliminating the African American population. Within the last decade, Ruth Bader Ginsburg famously described the Roe v. Wade decision as being intended to control population growth, "particularly growth in populations that we don't want to have too many of."[5]

In the early 1990s, the attorney for Roe, Ron Weddington, had urged then president-elect Bill Clinton that he needed a better educated, healthier, wealthier population in order to reform the country. To that end, he advised Clinton to "start immediately to eliminate the barely educated, unhealthy and poor segment of our country [through abortion.] . . . There, I've said it. It's what we all know is true, but we only whisper it."[6] The thirty million abortions at that time in the United States had, according to Weddington's measure, made the country much better, but at the cost of not just the lives lost but also the devastation of our cultural understanding of sex and responsibility. If the first duty of parenthood—allowing the child to live—has been eliminated, we can be sure every other human duty can be as well.

Sex without Meaning

The sexual revolution relies on this separation of sex from babies. It is not only conservative culture warriors who recognize this. In the first episode of the popular television

---

5   Kevin D. Williamson, "We Only Whisper It," *National Review*, September 24, 2014, https://www.nationalreview.com/2014/09/we-only-whisper-it-kevin-d-williamson/.

6   "How To Eliminate the Poor," *New Oxford Review*, October 2006, https://www.newoxfordreview.org/documents/how-to-eliminate-the-poor/.

show *Mad Men*, the character of Peggy is introduced to working-woman life on her first day at the office when veteran working woman Joan takes her to a doctor so she can be put on the Pill. The message was clear: separating sex from responsibility was the first step in becoming a modern woman. Peggy was now available for meaningless sex with men.

In order to mean nothing, sex has to remove constraints on the parties engaged in it. Any constraint would be an intolerable curb on the will. Our denial of the obvious connection between pregnancy and babies has resulted in much of the chaos and violence that plagues society today. Relationships between the sexes clearly exhibit this chaos, and violence is both the effect and the sustenance of this perverse ideology.

While *Mad Men* was a nuanced show, its standpoint was undeniably supportive of the advent of total sexual autonomy for women. But what has been the real-life legacy of this movement? Recently, the advice column over at *The Cut* published a letter that is some version of a complaint I've heard from numerous women. The woman writing in for advice described having been on nearly forty first dates in the past couple of years. At first, she thought casual dating was exactly what she needed. She tried casual relationships with various men, most of whom she shared chemistry with, but she realized that these relationships just made her feel badly about herself. "I was always so painfully aware of the fact that the only reason these guys were talking to me was because I was letting them sleep with me. . . . I felt like a sex doll. That might have been improved if the sex had been good, but it was mediocre at best. I tried to ignore the feelings and spice up the sex, but nothing worked."[7]

The lived reality of many women in today's dating swamp is that they are reduced to a tool for men's masturbation. The "remedy" of using the man in return seems less like empowerment and more like an infernal competition to see who can be made more miserable. It makes perfect sense that no one wants to introduce a baby into such a dismal dating scene. A baby requires all sorts of responsibility, sacrifice, devotion, permanence. That is to say, a baby requires real love, a love that the modern dating scene might try to mimic but cannot embody.

The promise of the sexual revolution was that sex can be meaningless. Indeed, it has to be meaningless to preserve our autonomy. If it has intrinsic meaning, independent of whatever we desire it to mean, then suddenly the threat of duties and responsibilities begins to infringe upon our autonomy.

This revolution has thrown human relationships into chaos from the inside out, most tragically the relationship between parent and child. A baby is a glaring, obtrusive manifestation of meaning interjected into our autonomy.

To maintain the illusion of sexual autonomy requires us to be at war with the science of basic human embryology, as well as our very selves: our bodies, minds, and emotions. This leaves women confused by the disconnect between the illusion and the reality. "This is casual, so why do I feel

---

7   Heather Havrilesky, "I Can't Do Casual," *The Cut*, May 15, 2019, https://www.thecut.com/2019/05/ask-polly-i-cant-do-casual. html.

intimately bonded to him? This is casual, so why do I feel used? This is casual, so why is a baby coming?"

A funny thing happens when we contort our thinking in a way that denies basic reality: people sometimes accidentally reason their way backward into the truth. This is what we saw when Alyssa Milano, in response to laws limiting the availability of abortion in 2019, called for sexual restraint in the form of a sex strike—the intended implication being that if men want sex, they'd better give us abortion, in case we were to get pregnant. The less intended implication was that were abortion not available, pregnancy and parenthood could be controlled through people practicing sexual restraint.

Another feminist tweet that went viral around the same time called for men to be responsible for both the women they have sex with and the children who might follow: "If abortion is illegal then men abandoning their child should also be illegal. If this was a permanent decision for me then it is for you as a father also."[8]

Both of these feminist declarations concede that because of the nature of sexual intimacy, and without the backstop of abortion, we all might have to realize our duties toward one another and our responsibilities to those to come. Not only does abortion fail to empower women, it exonerates men.

In his 2020 Netflix comedy special *Sticks and Stones*, Dave Chappelle pinpointed this dynamic with a darkly humorous bit that if women can unilaterally decide to have an abortion, then men can unilaterally decide not to provide for the child by skirting the burden of child support. His

---

8   Ricky Spanish (@5headshawtyyy), Twitter, May 12, 2019.

justification? "My money, my choice." He ended by saying that if women can kill a baby, then men should at least be able to abandon a baby. As the horror of the logic played out in the audience's mind, he muttered, "And if *I'm* wrong then perhaps *we're* wrong."

With the camouflage of abortion under threat, the lie of the sexually autonomous lifestyle and the deep injustice it has imposed on men, women, and children is exposed. We can somewhat cover up the emotional and psychological toll of casual sex, but we can't quite cover up a baby unless we get rid of it. As Anthony Esolen writes, "If the child lives, the mother's life will not be the same, because if we accept the principles that allow the child to live, none of our lives can be the same. There is no way to guarantee a world safe for the unborn child that is also a world of total sexual and economic autonomy. In any world in which autonomy is the highest ideal, the child—that incarnate sign of our dependence and existential poverty—must go."[9]

We might look at the modern dating world and ask ourselves if this lifestyle of delusion that we are fighting so hard to preserve is worth protecting at the price of innocent human lives. We cannot protect both.

The revolution was marketed as a reaction to a puritanical repression and hatred of the flesh. Setting aside the question of whether that was a fair presentation of the reality that preceded it, what we didn't anticipate was that the hedonism it ushered in is just a new type of hatred and distortion of

---

[9]   Anthony Esolen, "When Reason Does Not Suffice: Why Our Culture Still Accepts Abortion," *Public Discourse*, April 3, 2019, https://www.thepublicdiscourse.com/2019/04/50665/.

our flesh. We see this in the hatred of the flesh of posterity in the case of our unborn children but also in the ways we treat our own bodies. Without a deep and meaningful personal connection, without a core of love, we end up exaggerating and disfiguring the shell. A society that sees sex as meaningless obsesses over its particulars. We become, in the extreme, beasts and blow-up dolls prowling and posing.

But between the puritan and the hedonist there is also the way of the realist, for whom sex is neither bad nor meaningless but good and healthy and imbued with significance. The sexual realist knows that an act of total gift of self encompasses each lover's future, so he preserves sex for a context of deep love and permanence. The realist knows that if sex has no meaning, then neither does he, and that in asking us to sacrifice nothing, sexual autonomy costs us everything.

The New Woman

How has this harmful lifestyle been so effectively sold to us? In part, it has been glamorously packaged and presented for years through popular culture. It is well-trodden ground, but over the last few decades, TV shows notoriously went from family centric to anti-family—even in seemingly innocuous ways. The character of Rachel in the show *Friends* is introduced to the audience having just left her fiancé at the altar. He was a heel, but the real message conveyed throughout the series was that she created her own "family" of adorable urban friendships colored by easy sex and winsome jokes about the porn habits of the lovable male characters. Running away from marriage was a theme repeated in the movie

The Runaway Bride and sitcoms like *Suddenly Susan*, which also began with the premise of the main female character walking away from a fiancé to begin her single life in the city.

Probably the most iconic show depicting the new normal for women was the wildly popular *Sex and the City*. The show was like an irresistible cotton candy sales pitch to women. As it had an outsized influence on women's fashion, so too did it influence their behavior. Inevitably, there was a vast gulf between how Carrie's life seemed and how it translated into reality for her fans. Casual hook-ups after a night of drinking cosmos is decidedly less glamorous in real life. The material aspiration encouraged by the show was imprudent for all but an elite few. Even fewer can sustain the licentious sexuality without lasting physical and emotional wounds. The cultural physics of a growing hookup culture result in an increasing number of men who are coarse and entitled and women who feel used and discarded.

Sophisticated moderns think of *Leave it to Beaver* as a contrived reflection of a societally imposed and ultimately unfulfilling domesticity. But *Sex and the City* was the *Leave it to Beaver* of the sexual revolution: a glossy representation at odds with the sad reality on the ground. Our new conception of the good life for women as highly ambitious sexual libertines created a generation of Stepford single girls pantomiming a life of glamor that is as hollow as it is harmful.

The show's stepchild, *Girls*, was in many ways a response to this inauthenticity. While *Sex and the City* presented the appeal and glamor of the revolution, *Girls* contended squarely with the ugliness of it. But while reflecting the real sadness and complexity that stems from a hookup culture, *Girls*

reassured women that this is just the cost of their empowerment and an effect of their oppression. It acknowledged
the reality on the ground and supplied revolution-friendly
contextualization. Your wounds are real, as are your flaws,
and sometimes your life is a train wreck, *Girls* seemed to
affirm. The show acknowledged these things in a way *Sex
and the City* had not. However, the acknowledgment was
meant to lead not to a questioning of the suppositions which
had led the women there but for the sake of normalizing the
dysfunction through the authentic acknowledgment of it,
and a call to respond to it with even more radical feminism.
Sex and the City painted a fantasy, *Girls* at least called out the
fantasy. But instead of turning back toward the light, they
said to embrace the nihilism of their reality. It was a surren-
der rather than a call to something higher and better.

The Injustice of Identity Politics

The great sadness of woke ideology is the destructive harm
left in its wake and the circular way in which even the harm
causes us to further cling to the ideology. The effort to undermine and disrupt the natural cohesive threads of culture created generations of people wounded and seeking justice. But
rather than addressing those wounds, woke ideology seeks
to exploit them, using them to further their destruction by
stoking their rage.

A strange but very human side of suffering is that we can
react to it in exactly the wrong ways. There is a post-traumatic
tendency to become peevish in our tragedy, quick to take
offense by a good-willed but clumsily worded message of

sympathy, or to look askance at another's inadequate effort to relate. We can hold our traumas tightly, perpetually nursing them, and in so doing elevate ourselves to a special status where only we, who've suffered mightily, might enter. Our trauma can become both trophy and weapon.

One stark example among many in recent years was the feminist reaction to the accusations against Justice Brett Kavanaugh. The litany of personal testimonies of abuse recounted in response to the Kavanaugh hearings was heart-wrenching. In Christine Blasey Ford, survivors of abuse saw an everywoman wounded, wronged, and fearful. In Brett Kavanaugh, they saw their abuser, and in his skin color, his privilege. Emblematic of this phenomenon of identification was a *Washington Post* article titled "We are all Christine Ford. Or Brett Kavanaugh."[10]

The problem is, well, no. We are not. This is exactly the wrong way to think and speak if we're concerned with justice. A person's painful experience, grievous as it may be, tells us exactly nothing about Kavanaugh or the accuracy of Ford's accusation.

If we were to hear hundreds of stories of men recounting having endured false and defamatory accusations, would we then have had to side with Kavanaugh? Of course not. Other people's experiences are not evidence of an unrelated individual's guilt. Other people's experiences are just that.

---

[10]   Christine Emba, "We Are All Christine Ford. Or Brett Kavanaugh," *The Washington Post*, September 29, 2018, https://www.washingtonpost.com/opinions/we-are-all-christine-ford-or-brett-kavanaugh/2018/09/29/d19253ec-c36c-11e8-b338-a3289f6cb742_story.html..

If we want to talk about personal stories for the sake of growing in empathy or identifying and remedying a pattern of abuse in our society, then we can do that, but it needs to be outside of such contexts. It's a grave miscarriage of justice to apply a statistic or societal pattern to an individual in an effort to heap condemnation upon him.

A thought experiment: An African-American man from an inner city with a high crime rate is accused of a crime by a woman. There's no evidence and no corroboration, but there's a sincere-sounding accusation and compelling statistics of this type of crime from other men who fit his profile. He has flashes of anger as he defends himself. Soon stories start flooding social and other media from other women about their traumatic experiences with men from inner-city backgrounds who sound a lot like this particular man. They claim they see in this man a representation of their own assailant. They see themselves and their pain in the accuser. He represents to them the scourge of inner-city aggression. To not condemn him, they say, would be a slap in their faces and would reveal an unconscionable contempt for what they've endured. They storm the courthouse shouting stories of their pain and demanding this man bear the shame of it.

Would these stories at all be relevant to the question of his guilt or innocence? Wouldn't we be horrified if the African-American man were condemned, even if just in the court of public opinion, based not on the evidence of an allegation but rather on the mere fact of an accusation, compounded with sympathetic testimonies of people recounting their traumatic experiences with similarly profiled assailants? Wouldn't we find it sad but irrelevant that they'd had awful things happen to them, but also view it as quite prejudicial that their pain was being trotted out in order to convince people to rebuke this particular man whom they'd never known?

"But! But!" one might protest. "That would be offensive because black men have a privilege deficit!" That might be true, but first and foremost it's offensive because a basic principle of justice is that we don't determine an individual's guilt based on group identity, be it through societal patterns, statistics, or others' enumeration of their painful stories. We don't remedy irrational discrimination with more irrational discrimination.

Concerning the Kavanaugh hearings, a *New York Times* article evidenced the rage-fueled identity politics at the core of the response: "After a confirmation process where women all but slit their wrists, letting their stories of sexual trauma run like rivers of blood through the Capitol, the Senate still voted to confirm Judge Brett M. Kavanaugh to the Supreme Court. . . . Meanwhile, Senator Collins subjected us to a slow funeral dirge about due process and some other nonsense I couldn't even hear through my rage headache as she announced on Friday she would vote to confirm Judge Kavanaugh. Her mostly male colleagues applauded her."[11]

In other words, the experiences of women who are wholly unconnected to this accusation were sufficiently relevant, due process is nonsense, and Senator Susan Collins's reasonable

---

[11]   Alexis Grenell, "White Women, Come Get Your People," *The New York Times*, October 6, 2018, https://www.nytimes.com/2018/10/06/opinion/lisa-murkowski-susan-collins-kavanaugh.html.

words should be dismissed because of the sex of those who applauded her. Identity politics will not tolerate reason.

To associate justice for the individual with the collective is to abandon justice entirely. Justice doesn't praise or condemn people or evaluate their honesty or complicity based on being part of a group, or by having a certain skin color, or by belonging to a certain economic class, or by being a woman or a man. If we're concerned about justice, we need to apply just principles, otherwise the price of being woke is that our eyes are wide open but our minds are fast asleep.

That Kavanaugh was confirmed wasn't a slap in the face of all survivors of assault. He wasn't confirmed because sexual assault doesn't matter or because Collins was anti-woman. He was confirmed because by any standard of justice, one person's uncorroborated accusation unaccompanied by evidence ought to be insufficient to destroy or derail another person of any color, sex, or background.

If we want our stories of pain, no matter how numerous and severe, to become evidence of another's guilt, then what we want isn't justice but vengeance. What we want isn't a societal remedy but a scapegoat. And what we are guided by looks less like principle and more like fanaticism.

Without a universal principle, "justice" becomes preference dependent on historical interpretation from a perspective that is ahistorical. It requires unjust means to achieve the desired end. It also seeks to provide cover for wounds rather than addressing the wound itself. In fact, so many of the wounds which lead people to this tribalism are rooted in circumstances both celebrated and encouraged by woke culture: the dissolution of the family as the primary cell of human society, the rejection of sexual mores that served to protect the health and integrity of the dynamics between men and women, and the uncompromising support for abortion which has left millions of women with a depth and pain of remorse that they are not allowed to acknowledge. They are wounds and scars inflicted on a society in denial of the fundamental reality of the embodied human person.

Gnosticism

We long to have dominion over our bodies, to let our wills triumph over them. We imagine we might be freer by considering the body to be a meaningless cage that we can manipulate in defiance of any real meaning imbued by it. Behind the door of many modern errors hides the old heresy of Gnosticism.

The denial of an intelligible human nature leads to a distinct chaos of people at war with their own bodies. In order to say that I can be *anything*, I have to in fact mean *nothing*, for to be *something* always excludes being something else. And this is ultimately the point of queer theory—to disrupt normativity and to deconstruct bodily reality. James Lindsay writes that the goal "is to create a single sex/gender/sexual identity that more or less describes everyone (or, everyone good, according to queer Theory) as queer. . . . Queer Theory isn't necessarily explicitly trying to create one 'right' sex/gender/sexual identity for everyone so much as it is trying to remove any meaning or significance from any stable sex/

gender/sexual identity category at all, leaving queer identity as the default."[12]

In 1993, Pope St. John Paul II wrote, "A freedom which claims to be absolute ends up treating the human body as raw datum, devoid of any meaning and moral values until freedom has shaped it in accordance with its design."[13] The effort to detach ourselves from the meaning of our bodies is exhibited in trans-activism, in the meaninglessness of sex, and also in the elimination of the significance of male and female difference. One or the other must go: we either give up our identity as autonomous willing agents or we give up our identity as being intimately tied to our biology.

It is difficult to consistently deny objective bodily meaning, and its denial leads to all sorts of monstrosities. The implications of a denial of bodily meaning were of great concern to St. John Paul II, who was familiar with the violations of the body carried out under the banner of the reductive materialism of socialism. In concentration camps, in addition to the horrors of genocide, prisoners were also experimented on in the name of science. Various types of bacteria were injected into their bodies causing anything from painful open sores to infection and agonizing death.

As we enter into this third generation of the sexual revolution, the unraveling Unwin warned us about, and the irrational denial of bodily reality, can be seen starkly.

In 2018, the best picture Oscar award went to a film about a woman having intercourse with a fish. Too much can be

---

[12]   James Lindsay, "Authentic," *New Discourses*, June 25, 2020, https://newdiscourses.com/tftw-authentic/.

[13]   Pope St. John Paul II, *Veritatis Splendor*, p. 48.

made of any one cultural moment, but this one seemed fitting. You can almost hear the sexual wokeness in the writing sessions: "I see your 'throuple' and I raise you amphibian sex!" Onward to the next frontier.

The movie was aptly titled *The Shape of Water*, which is clever of course because water has no shape. It is ever-fluid, ever-changing—the perfect mascot for an ideology that rejects any restrictions of nature and instead bends its knee to unbridled desire. This war is finally a war on the body, on form, on a nature imbued with purposes and norms.

It is not that we no longer believe there is a human good, it is that we've convinced ourselves that our highest good is the fulfillment of our individual desires as the expression of our autonomy. It is a highest good without any definition or meaning. But autonomy divorced from nature sets up a power struggle of competing wills which has violence as its end.

This elevation of personal autonomy forces us to relegate questions of how we ought to live, questions which affect us most deeply, into the sphere of private opinion. We take our desires for connection, love, and sex, and rather than treat them with moral seriousness, we move stupidly through the materialist paths presented to us with our autonomy in our wallets.

In the marketplace of persons, everything is a negotiation. Someone's currency might be money, power, sex appeal. We commodify persons through casual sex, halftime shows, porn, prostitution, slavery, and they are all of one piece, varying in degree but not in kind. We have trained ourselves and each other that a person is a thing to be used according to our desire. Something I can buy is something I can own and have the right to do with as I wish. And something I have a potential right to becomes something I can rationalize taking. The rule of desire over time becomes too formidable for the paper-thin buffer of consent.

This is a cesspool in which all participants become bored, miserable, and eventually experience various levels of abuse. We seem to be waking up to the fact that we are drowning. A person is not meant to endlessly tread water; eventually he must acknowledge that he is exhausted and getting nowhere before the despair of his situation overcomes him.

In a recent *New York Times* piece, a woman makes her case for becoming a secular celibate. In thinking through her decision, she speculates, "Maybe it is also an empowerment thing, that I don't need attention from a man at all, that I have myself. All of my sleepless nights staying up crying, wondering if he's ever going to call me again, if he still likes me, do I have worth outside of my vagina — all these doubts just left when I quit dealing with men. I have never been happier."[14]

Her rejection of the opposite sex tracks along with other recent trends from people who are shrugging off what little value they see left in the marketplace of sexual exchange. Love and happiness seem to many like the leftover mist from a children's story. Pleasure becomes more elusive the more common and loveless its pursuit is, and no one in today's autonomy really needs someone else for that anyway. In this

---

[14]   Sanam Yar, "I Quit Dating Entirely," *The New York Times*, January 20, 2020, https://www.nytimes.com/2020/01/20/style/no-sex -celibacy.html.

context, rejection of the other sex seems entirely reasonable. Even fashion is increasingly becoming asexual or androgynous. In the ever-fluid battle of the sexes, not only do we reject the other, but we eventually reject ourselves.

In its impulse, it is an act of self-preservation. We tell ourselves, "This is better, I am relieved, and in comparison to that old exhausting norm of treading water in place, this feels like the good life." But life spent alone clinging to a raft, while less exhausting, is still unfulfilling.

When something is true, we can arrive at it from multiple angles. Conversely, when something is wrong, we might perceive some aspect of its wrongness in all sorts of ways. But like so many reactions today, ours tend to be more escape than solution.

This model of will and domination cannot contain, nor can it traverse, the vast ocean that is real human love. Instead we become increasingly mechanized, smaller and more atomized, swiping, blinking into screens, robotic and battery operated. The end result of the will unbound by nature is not a superhuman but a subhuman.

We are drawn to water; it has long been a symbol for mystery, life, rebirth. But we are not amphibians. Understandably, many are reaching for a raft, rejecting the water entirely. But if we squint past our present, we might see that there is another way of being, that we need not reject the water and wander the desert, nor cling endlessly to a raft. We might see that there is a seaside and a ship and another way of living altogether. A life not without struggle but with the struggle to be beautifully embodied and intimately human—to be a man, to be a woman—and to reject as misery the carnival pantomime of either.

9

Thought and Speech Control

When Jewish philosopher Hannah Arendt attended the trial of Adolph Eichmann, the architect of the Holocaust, she expected to see in him some incarnation of evil. Instead, what she found was more disconcerting: he seemed ordinary, even banal. There was nothing about him that would lead an observer to detect the monstrous and demonic atrocities which he had orchestrated. She did discern something else in him. "It was not stupidity but a curious, quite authentic inability to think."[1] Eichmann seemed to Arendt to be shallow, following ideas to their logical end without examining or questioning their premises.

Arendt did not intend her characterization to be interpreted as commentary upon Eichmann's IQ. Nor did she mean to suggest that he was not capable of critical thinking. Commenting on Arendt's experience, Jack Kerwick notes, "Rather, her point was that Eichmann showed no will to think beyond the clichés—the memes, bumper sticker slogans, and hashtags—of his day. . . . It is crucial for the

---

[1]   Jack Kerwick, "The Great UnReason of 2020: The 'Curious, but Quite Authentic, Inability to Think,'" *FrontPage*, May 7, 2020, https://cms.frontpagemag.com/fpm/2020/05/great-unreason -2020-curious-quite-authentic-jack-kerwick.

reader to recognize that the phenomenon that she witnessed in Eichmann she knew was one that is endemic to human beings generally."[2]

What we are left with is the dreadful realization that there was nothing unique at all about Eichmann. The ability to think critically is an essential component in preparing ourselves to resist evil-doing. Relinquishing this distinctively human aspect of our nature leaves us susceptible to the whims of a mob, or of a ruler, or of our own inclinations. Sloganeering is essential to propaganda and ideology; as such, it is a powerful tool when coupled with a decline in critical thinking.

Critical Thinking vs Critical Theory

As the sociologist Unwin discovered, there is at least a correlative relationship between increased sexual freedom and the devolution of thought. The second characteristic of woke ideology shows us that the connection between the elevation of the will and the rejection of reason is more than merely correlative. If we want the fact of our willing something to be sufficient to justify our pursuit of it, then we will have to suspend thinking critically about our actions.

The rejection of reason and nature has taken root as well through the replacement of critical thinking with critical theory. The latter has been the engine of academic thought for decades, and its methods pervade every discipline and subject.

---

2   Ibid.

Critical thinking, in the classical liberal tradition, relies on the reality that we are rational animals, able to use our abilities to observe the world, discern universal principles, and make normative evaluations. We can determine, generally, what *ought* to be from what *is* and develop, challenge, and refine arguments by evaluating the premises and logic involved. Through intellectual rigor, we can more fully own our ideas and evaluate the validity and veracity of the ideas of others with the goal of arriving at truth.

Essential to critical thinking is the discipline to understand the best opposing arguments to one's position. St. Thomas Aquinas exemplified this in the *Summa Theologica*. The Angelic Doctor first poses a question and then raises the strongest arguments against the answer he will ultimately give. Even after giving his *sed contra*, Aquinas makes the best of each objection in light of his understanding. Thus, only after carefully and thoroughly considering every worthy opposing position does he show the reader how each argument in opposition bears some fatal flaw.

In modern parlance, we call this *steel manning*. Whereas *straw manning* is the fallacy of arguing against the weakest position of your opponent, *steel manning* is arguing against the best possible opposing argument, even beyond what they present themselves.

Implicit in the rigor of critical thinking is the preeminence it gives to the search for truth and an acknowledgment that our desire to be right can tend to corrupt the integrity of that search.

In contrast, the purpose of critical theory is to support the ideology of cultural Marxism and churn out activists rather than to arrive at truth. To engage in critical theory is to filter all humanity through the lens of power for the sake of reversing the power dynamic of the dominant oppressor class. Power, not truth, is preeminent for the critical theorist. That many of us do not realize the distinction between these two methods leads to a lot of frustration. The great strength of the critical thinker is that she eagerly invites criticism. The great weapon of the theorists is that they eagerly provide criticism but never invite it. One side thinks the norm is still critical thought, but the ideologues know we are engaged, not in discourse, but in a power play.

This way of dismantling critical thought has been, and continues to be, enacted through the enshrining of critical theory within the majority of Western education. By applying a filter of suspicion to every field of study, no work of art, historical event, or reasoned argument can be seen objectively. There is always a power dynamic to uncover and to dismantle. Everything becomes political.

This is not a small matter relegated to the ivory tower with merely academic ramifications. Hannah Arendt saw that shallow sloganeering and an unwillingness to think can lead ordinary people to otherwise unimaginable monstrosities. In the riots of 2020, we saw it exhibited in the inability of Progressives to effectively and unequivocally denounce the violence and destruction. If truth is a function of power, unjust actions become far more palatable if they can be understood to be advantageous to the right cause.

Compelled Speech, Compelled Thought

For the woke, the person with the oppressed positionality has greater insight and a right to silence the person in the position of dominance. An example of this is the common refrain that if you do not have a uterus, you cannot speak about abortion. This used to be considered an *ad hominem* fallacy—dismissing an argument based on the identity of the arguer. For example, it would be an *ad hominem* to say a white abolitionist cannot speak against slavery, or that a woman cannot say that men should not watch pornography, or that a celibate person cannot say that marital infidelity is bad.

According to the woke, it is not the weight of the argument but the skin color, gender, or sexuality of the speaker which determines the rightness or wrongness of the speech. And even then, having the oppressed identity only gives credence to the argument if the speaker espouses the correct ideology. A white man who defends woke ideology need not defer to a black woman who rejects it.

Multiple messages emerged in the aftermath of the horrific videos of a police officer with a knee on George Floyd's neck. "Listen more; talk less" was a common one. White people were urged to "take a seat and *listen*." These messages were not surprising, and considered on their own, there is certainly value in listening to a community that has experienced harms particular to them.

But this time they were accompanied by a new, and contradictory, rallying cry. Rather than telling white people to just be silent and listen, the additional message was that white silence is violence. No longer is it enough to be not racist, now is the time to be vocally anti-racist. That both messages (be silent and silence is violence) were repeatedly proffered even while contradicting one another is reflective of the chaotic discord in which we all live. The movement wants those with white privilege to repent *but also to remain unforgiven.* The privileged must express sorrow and shame in the face of their privilege, while also cowering in silence on account of their privilege. The combination of the reigning admonitions that "words are violence" and "silence is violence" leaves only one remaining possibility: compulsory ideologically-approved speech.

The norm shifted from giving people the benefit of the doubt unless they prove us wrong to assuming everyone with white skin is racist and the best they can do is to publicly ally themselves with the Black Lives Matter ideology.

"Black lives matter" is a true and good statement, one that no decent person can deny. Black lives matter because of our common humanity and the dignity of the person made in the image of God. But the movement of Black Lives Matter is explicitly and aggressively neo-marxist. From their statement of beliefs page: "We disrupt the Western-prescribed nuclear family structure requirement. . . . We foster a queer-affirming network. When we gather, we do so with the intention of freeing ourselves from the tight grip of heteronormative thinking."[3] To propose that the solution for the plight of people of color is to advance queer theory and

---

[3]   https://blacklivesmatter.com/what-we-believe/. Access date 07/01/20. Was subsequently removed some months later.

disrupt the family unit is, frankly, insanity. But affirmation of this movement's platform is the new benchmark required to assert our anti-racism *bona fides*.

Black Lives Matter cofounder Patrisse Cullors said in a video from 2015 that she and her fellow organizers are "trained Marxists."[4] In his book *How to Be an Antiracist*, author Ibram X. Kendi claims capitalism is essentially racist, and racism is essentially capitalist. He writes, "They were birthed together from the same unnatural causes, and they shall one day die together from unnatural causes."[5] In order to not be racist now, we, apparently, must embrace alternative sexual lifestyles, support disrupting the nuclear family, and endorse socialism.

Disciplining Heretics

The lurch toward militancy in 2020 America means a person is far less free to question these ideological tenets and tactics. When a UCLA professor refused to cancel finals for students of color after the George Floyd videos, he was doxed by students and put on a mandatory leave of absence.[6] Pro

---

4   Yaron Steinbuch, "Black Lives Matter co-founder describes herself as 'trained Marxist,'" New York Post, June 25, 2020, https://nypost.com/2020/06/25/blm-co-founder-describes-herself-as-trained-marxist/.

5   Kendi X Abrams, *How to Be an Antiracist* (Independently published, 2020), p. 163.

6   James Varney, "Professor suspended for refusing to give some special treatment in wake of Floyd's death, defended," *The Washington Times*, June 10, 2020, https://www.washingtontimes.com/news/2020/jun/10/gordon-klein-ucla-professor-suspended-doling-speci/.

soccer player Aleksander Katai was released from his team
not for anything he did but because his wife criticized the
BLM movement on social media.[7] A former Canadian cab-
inet minister lost three jobs after saying that he didn't think
Canada was a racist country.[8]

Even among religious groups, the dogmas of the woke
are growing sacrosanct. Such was the case for a Florida State
University student, Jack Denton, who discovered that free
speech did not apply to criticism of BLM. In a private group
chat of Catholic Student Union members, when links were
sent around by fellow Catholics in support BLM, Denton let the group know that they support things that are
anti-Catholic, such as transgenderism and abortion. When
some students took offense, he wrote to his fellow Catholics, "If I stay silent while my brothers and sisters may be
supporting an organization that promotes grave evils, I have
sinned through my silence. I love you all, and I want us all
to be aware of the truth."[9]

---

[7]   Sam McEvoy, "LA Galaxy release midfielder Aleksander Katai fol-
       lowing 'racist' posts made by his wife on social media that called
       for protestors to be 'killed' during Black Lives Matter Move-
       ment," *Daily Mail*, June 5, 2020, https://www.dailymail.co.uk/
       sport/sportsnews/article-8392937/LA-Galaxy-release-Aleksandar-
       Katai-following-racist-posts-wife-social-media.html.

[8]   Peter Zimonjic, "Stockwell Day exits CBC commentary role, cor-
       porate posts after comments about racism in Canada," *CBC*, June
       3, 2020, https://www.cbc.ca/news/politics/stockwell-day-systemic
       -racism-canada-1.5597550.

[9]   Allie Langhofer, "A Student Punished for Privately Sharing Reli-
       gious Views," *Alliance Defending Freedom*, July 14, 2020, https://
       adflegal.org/blog/student-punished-privately-sharing-religious
       -views?fbclid=IwAR2KYI4bKJsr0qnpe58H9oHzcSElJcTDVAT
       pGxBu4ZGxkHJ_3CUucOhykIQ.

It could have ended there, but one student leaked his comment to the student government association, of which Denton served as student senate president. A fellow student senator claimed Denton's words showed an intent to hurt other students emotionally and physically. Some senators claimed they felt unsafe with him as a result. A vote to remove him came in with a majority in favor of his removal but which fell short of the necessary two-thirds majority.

A Change.org petition for his removal was circulated saying Denton was transphobic and racist. Senators who had voted against Denton's removal were pressured by their fellow students to change their votes, lest they too be accused of transphobia and racism. Denton, who had served with distinction and was seemingly well-regarded by the others before this, was removed after a revote.

In a private Catholic group chat, Denton respectfully gave salient information about basic Catholic moral teaching and was deemed to be beyond the pale. His replacement, Ahmed Omar Daraldik, was discovered to have made expletive laden, derogatory, anti-semitic remarks on social media posts. Daraldik was not removed, nor was cause for his removal taken to a vote.

Denton's case has been taken up by the Alliance Defending Freedom non-profit. While a US district judge ruled that Denton should not be reinstated, FSU's internal court system ruled in favor of the exercise of free speech and has since reinstated him. Though the outcome was just, Denton discovered in the process what many others have—that Catholic teaching can now be classified as unsafe hate speech. But even if one cowers at such tactics and parrots progressive talking points, there is no guarantee that she will find satisfaction with the militant woke. Privilege will always make a person suspect. Celebrated author and race counselor Robin D'Angelo writes, "I believe that white progressives cause the most daily damage to people of color. I define a white progressive as any white person who thinks he or she is not racist, or is less racist, or in the 'choir,' or already 'gets it.'"[10]

DiAngelo goes on to say that we must insist white Progressives engage in ongoing self-examination of their internalized racism and receive training in anti-racist education and doctrines. Even at the end of this lifelong endeavor, if a white Progressive is told that she is a racist, any defense she gives against such a charge will only be further proof of its veracity. Denial of racism is proof of racism. It is a lifelong futile effort of self-flagellation without redemption.

Not only is there no hope on a personal level, there is no real reconciliation among groups either. A white person who promises ongoing examination of her privilege and commits to lifelong activism might be accepted for now (though still remaining an oppressor for life), but the privileged group as a whole cannot be. No group will ever be monolithic; there will always be disparate voices. As long as there are voices who do not give dogmatic assent to the woke, there will be no reconciliation among groups. But reconciliation was never the endgame anyway.

---

[10] Robin DiAngelo, *White Fragility: Why It's So Hard for White People to Talk About Racism* (Beacon Press, 2018), introduction.

Concept Creep and Microaggressions

Musa al-Gharbi, a sociologist at Columbia University, has written compellingly about our evolving understanding of racism. In the past, accusations of racism were reserved for overtly racist acts, bigoted views, or racial animus. Such acts and expressions of prejudice are far less common now, as well as far less acceptable. Both of these developments, al-Gharbi notes, are unquestionably positive, but he notes another development alongside this progress: our concept of what we consider racist is ever-expanding. "As a function of the increased social capital at stake when accusations of racism are made, and the diminishing opportunities to leverage that capital by 'calling out' obvious cases of racism, . . . it is now possible to qualify as 'racist' on the basis of things like microaggressions and implicit attitudes."[11]

A screaming match over accusations of racism at a New York City education council meeting illustrates this concept creep well. The meeting was already contentious due to a disagreement over academic screenings. Some council members insisted on terminating them to better integrate schools, while others argued that screenings enabled teachers to teach to similarly positioned academic levels, resulting in more effective classrooms. All members were advocating for better school integration but differed on how best to implement it.

---

[11]   Musa al-Gharbi, "who gets to define what's 'racist?'" *contexts* (blog), May 15, 2020, https://contexts.org/blog/who-gets-to-define-whats -racist/.

One woke white woman, the group's past president, Robin Broshi, accused another council member, Thomas Wrocklage, of being guilty of racism. His transgression? At a prior meeting, he had been holding the nephew of a visiting friend (who happened to be black), and the sight of a white man holding a black child was too much for Broshi to tolerate. She erupted, "It *hurts* people when they see a white man bouncing a brown baby on their lap and they don't know the context! That is harmful! It makes people cry!"[12]

An open letter signed by dozens of parents was sent to the council president complaining that "a white man displayed a black baby on his lap on more than one occasion." The open letter claimed that any person of color would have suffered emotional injury witnessing this scene which was "shocking, disgusting, offensive, and racially incendiary."[13] The council president was threatened with removal for not controlling Wrocklage's racism. Broshi upbraided him, demanding that he read Ibram Kendi.

The woke have a supply and demand problem. The demand to uncover racism is at an all-time high while the supply of racial transgressions is at a low, creating a fervor and hysteria to convince people to see racism where it is not. Robin DiAngelo evidences this: "I am often asked if I think the younger generation is less racist. No, I don't. In some ways, racism's adaptations over time are more sinister than concrete rules such as Jim Crow." Further, DiAngelo notes, "The simplistic idea that racism is limited to individual intentional acts committed by unkind people is at the root of virtually all white defensiveness on this topic."[14]

Progress, according to DiAngelo, is not enacted by just laws and reductions in acts of racism, because there still lies within each white person's heart a whole host of unproveable racial animus. In her unfalsifiable dogmas, just laws and just behavior do not reflect improved race relations, they only obscure the more sinister racism beneath the surface.

It is undoubtable that racism has existed in widespread ways, and it is equally undoubtable that it remains a problem today; acts of racial injustice remind us of that brutal reality. But stoking a perception that it has morphed into something invisible and omnipresent is destructive in two ways. First, with a veneer compassion, white Progressives are cementing a perception that people of color are less able to move forward in life and have less agency than white people. Misplaced pity insinuates inferiority. Secondly, this thinking directly reifies and amplifies racial animus. Obsessing over race relations by constantly searching for the slightest transgression, even invisible and unconscious transgressions, places entire societies on edge and brainwashes people to see nothing but race in every daily interaction they have, a sure

---

[14]   Robin DiAngelo, *White Fragility: Why It's So Hard for White People to Talk About Racism* (Beacon Press, 2018), p. 50.

recipe for stoking racial tensions; people will see things that aren't there, misread intentions, and assume the worst.

Musa al-Gharbi writes that a recent metanalysis on micro-aggressions found little empirical substantiation for the claims of harm that are advanced in critical race theory literature. Yet the harm caused by heightened perceptions of racism, discrimination, racialized violence, and racial inequality were demonstrated by an abundance of research: "There are very well-established and highly-adverse impacts on the psychological (and even physical) well-being of people of color when they perceive more racism, racial inequality, and discrimination. That is, we have not (yet) been able to empirically verify that microaggressions are typically harmful, nor have we been able to effectively measure the extent of that harm. . . . However, we have ample reason to believe that sensitizing people to better perceive and to take greater offense at these 'slights' actually would cause harm."[15]

Loving the Sin, Hating the Sinner

One common refrain from the Right is that the notion of Progressive tolerance seems to consistently contain a double standard of "tolerance for me but not for thee." Consider the demand for tolerance of any sexual deviation versus the militant cancelling and intolerance extended to advocates of traditional sexual morality. To any student of Marcuse, the

---

[15]   Musa al-Gharbi, "who gets to define what's 'racist?'" *contexts* (blog), May 15, 2020, https://contexts.org/blog/who-gets-to-define-whats-racist/.

one-sidedness is not a partisan blind spot; rather, this double standard is by design. It is a feature, not a flaw.

The word *tolerance* signifies something neutral—a certain detachment from one's own beliefs in order to get along peacefully with those who hold other beliefs. A tolerant society on its face seems like it should be one in which all people try to live and let live, with plenty of space for disagreement. If that were all it was, then we could expect it to be extended in all directions without partiality, except perhaps in extreme cases. But we sense this is not the entire picture.

The cultural imperative of tolerance was always a sophisticated Trojan horse that leads to an attack against truth. Society was groomed to embrace moral relativism through the exhortation to be tolerant and the accusation of judgementalism.

Before most people on the right were deemed bigots, the more common accusation directed at cultural conservatives was that they were "judgmental." This epithet was deployed in the culture wars early and often to great effect, especially on a weakening and waning mainstream Christianity. Many were understandably fazed by it—after all, Christianity preaches mercy, and the image of a finger-wagging Christian scold is unattractive. Most of us can easily imagine this church lady either because we've seen those *Saturday Night Live* skits and a thousand other examples of that archetype in movies or because we have encountered such a person to some degree in real life. But there is a too-quickly dismissed distinction as old as the Church that says we can judge an act but not the heart of the actor, otherwise known as "hate the sin, love the sinner." For centuries, Christians were told to refrain from judging our neighbor's heart, even if he had clearly done something wrong. Perhaps he was reacting to a deep wound, or he was misled or confused or suffering in some way that mitigates his culpability. We cannot know the exact state of another's soul at any given time, and that state often changes over time. Nor is it our business to know who they are now, or what they became after the act.

But somewhere along the road of thinning theology and increasingly demagogic secularism, modern Christianity absorbed and internalized the message that "do not judge" in particular is synonymous with "do not acknowledge that acts can be right or wrong" in general. So successful has been the effort to brand morally normative statements as judgmental that many shepherds have become cowardly and their flock apathetic.

Nowhere is this more pronounced than with the hot-button issues surrounding sexuality. An especially effective tactic has been to redefine love and hate around support or opposition to sexual mores. "Love" today demands the rejection of sexual moral norms. The effect has been exactly the opposite of what we might have supposed. By no longer judging the *acts* of men, we have morphed into people who can *only* judge the *hearts* of men. We love the sin and hate the sinner—which is a much more insidiously judgmental posture.

Once an objective moral measure is abandoned, we are left only to measure the subjective intent of another person. One way this manifests itself is in the implications of trans ideology. After the unsexing of public bathrooms, the next barrier is unsexing all gendered spaces. There is no longer a principle available to object to boys in girls' locker rooms, including shared showers, at public schools. In practice, how will we distinguish between the sincere boy with gender dysphoria and the insincere boy who might be a predator, or at least taking advantage of the situation? Without drawing the line at the very clear measure that holds a boy to be a boy no matter what he thinks or says, we are left with the very unclear measure of reading souls. Is this boy really a girl trapped in a boy's body and therefore not a threat to the biological girls in the locker room? Or is this boy perhaps confused but with typically male drives? Or maybe is he dissembling and predatory? This same issue will repeat itself in women's shelters, prisons, dormitories, and on and on. Without an objective standard, we have to guess at intent.

The acceptance and spread of relativism leads to the inevitable consequence of tolerance becoming a one-way street. Identity politics is a chief beneficiary and proponent of this campaign to brand proponents of an objective morality as judgmental. The incoherence baked into moral relativism made mutual tolerance unsustainable. At some point, what at first is viewed as a legal right to be tolerated eventually demands to be affirmed as a moral right to be embraced. Any view which makes exclusive claims on truth that does not cater to this newly perceived moral right cannot be tolerated. Traditional morality will not be debated; rather, the intent of those who advocate for it must be demonized.

Repressive Tolerance

In his influential essay "Repressive Tolerance," Marcuse rejects the ideals of free speech and mutual toleration and instead writes of the imperative to discriminate against anyone on the wrong side of revolution. "The hierarchical structure of society is inherently violent toward the progress of society. Therefore, any violence introduced by the repressed in the name of progress is not the introduction of violence but the just reaction to a violent system."[16] Not only is intolerance to the revolution's enemies justified, it is necessary, even just.

Tolerance, Marcuse would go on to say, cannot be maintained equally because it works to the benefit of the powerful and encourages the oppressed to feel a false level of equality. Though this might seem unjust in practice, Marcuse assured those he was radicalizing that it was necessary for the sake of historical progress. He continues, "Since when is history made in accordance with ethical standards? To start applying them at this point where the oppressed rebel against the oppressors, the have-nots against the haves is serving the cause of actual violence by weakening the protest against it.[17]

The influence of Marcuse and the Frankfurt School is alive and well within the contemporary woke movement. In guiding the manner in which social justice should be implemented in schools, race counselors Özlem Sensoy and DiAngelo outline an example of how to employ repressive

---

[16]   Herbert Marcuse, "Repressive Tolerance," Marcuse.org, accessed November 11, 2020, https://www.marcuse.org/herbert/publications/1960s/1965-repressive-tolerance-fulltext.html.

[17]   Ibid.

tolerance tactics while teaching anti-bullying lessons about sexual identities in a classroom. At the end of a presentation, a hypothetical situation is raised as an instructive on how to apply discrimination for the sake of the ideology. In the hypothetical, a student raises her hand and states that she has a moral disagreement with a certain sexual lifestyle choice and believes she should not be required to express acceptance of it. The instructor allows her to finish and thanks her for sharing her perspective, then moves on to the next comment. According to Sensoy and DiAngelo, this is an incorrect way of handling the situation, as it allows the classroom to be subjected to oppressive dominant narratives and microaggressions. Instead, the dominant voice expressing traditional sexual norms must be silenced:

> When—in service to "fairness"—instructors give equal time to dominant narratives, we reinforce problematic discursive effects by legitimizing the idea that the conversation is equalizing only when it also includes dominant voices. This is why we have come to deny equal time to all narratives in our classrooms. Our intentions in doing so are to correct the existing power imbalances by turning down the volume on dominant narratives; to make space for dominant narratives in order to be "fair" assumes that these imbalances don't already exist or that equality of airtime is all that is needed to correct them. Because of this, we believe that restricting dominant narratives is actually more equalizing.[18]

---

18   Ozlem Sensoy and Robin DiAngelo, "Respect Differences? Chal-

A free exchange of ideas was never a woke goal. A principled application of justice was never the intention.

This is how radicals, including Marcuse, endorsed the terrorism tactics of the Weather Underground bombings. It is easy to see the connection here to our current cancel culture, as well as the vandalism and rioting that is considered unquestionable when done by a members of an oppressed group. As Ibram X. Kendi writes, "The only remedy to past discrimination is present discrimination."[19]

Understanding the tactic of repressive tolerance helps make sense of articles like the *Washington Post* piece entitled "Why Can't We Hate Men?" In it the author tells men that based on their biology, "don't run for office. Don't be in charge of anything. Step away from the power. We got this. And please know that your crocodile tears won't be wiped away by us anymore. We have every right to hate you. You have done us wrong. #BecausePatriarchy. It is long past time to play hard for Team Feminism. And win."[20]

It is also why the Toronto head of Black Lives Matter felt perfectly within her bounds to write a racist screed, using an alternative gender-neutral spelling for "human"

---

lenging the Common Guidelines in Social Justice Educatio," *Democracy and Education*, Vol. 22, no. 1, https://robindiangelo.com/wp-content/uploads/2016/01/Challenging-the-Common-Guidelines-in-Social-Justice-Education.pdf.

[19] Ibram X. Kendi, "Ibram X. Kendi defines what it means to be an antiracist," Penguin, June 9, 2020, https://www.penguin.co.uk/articles/2020/june/ibram-x-kendi-definition-of-antiracist/.

[20] Suzanna Danuta Walters, "Why Can't We Hate Men?" *The Washington Post*, June 8, 2018, https://www.washingtonpost.com/opinions/why-cant-we-hate-men/2018/06/08/f1a3a8e0-6451-11e8-a69c-b944de66d9e7_story.html.

in a now-deleted post, "Whiteness is not humxness. In fact, white skin is sub-humxn. All phenotypes exist within the black family and white [people] are a genetic defect of blackness."[21]

The goal is not a humanizing equality for all under the eyes of the law but a power reversal.

Cult Behavior

While the mob is the natural habitat for the woke, the movement adopts the psychological tactics of a cult. It is true that a great many on the Left remain reasonable and able to see things from other viewpoints, but the deeper into the ideology one gets, the more illiberal and closed-off one tends to become.

There are well-trodden comparisons between the woke and fundamentalist religions: rejection of critical thinking, demand for total adherence to dogmas, ritualistic shaming, and rejection of transgressors. Human beings have instincts to religiosity, and in the void left by our dismissal of God, we tend to erect false and harsh gods out of ourselves.

We want to be part of a great drama or a grand narrative that gives meaning to our lives, our sufferings, our daily efforts. Postmodern woke culture strips us of grand narratives and fractures each narrative into personal preference with no connection to ultimate meaning. We have narratives, but they are narratives of futility. People who look at

---

21   Alex Griswold, "Black Lives Mattr Leader: White People are 'Sub-Human,' 'Genetic Defects,'" *Mediaite*, February 13, 2017, https://www.mediaite.com/online/black-lives-matter-leader-white-people-are-sub-human-genetic-defects/.

this honestly tend to find the nihilism too much to bear. Others distract themselves from the meaninglessness with bread and circuses. Others carve out a sort of religion from their politics, but it is a religion united not by a grand narrative but by a common enemy. It is the cyclical finding and denouncing of a scapegoat without ever arriving at the Innocent Victim.

The woke will not take lightly their being defined as a religion, much less as a cult. But indoctrination into ideology often adopts cult-like tactics in its evangelization. Now we will consider some characteristics of cults and how they are incorporated by the woke.

Unquestionable dogmas

Critical thinking is discouraged. The replacement of critical thinking with critical theory abandons as a value any questioning of its tenets and expresses a hostility to reason, discourse, and free thought. Unfalsifiable and inarguable dogma reign.

Adherents can never be good enough

You must confess your privilege, become formed in woke doctrines through reeducation, and commit to a lifelong effort to resist your original sin of whiteness (an ultimately impossible task). Author James Lindsay writes, "You must be an ally but accept that you will always do your allyship wrong."[22]

---

[22]   James Lindsay, "The Cult Dynamics of Wokeness," *New Discourses*, June 6, 2020, https://newdiscourses.com/2020/06/cult-dynamics -wokeness/.

Isolation from people outside the group, even family and friends

There is no more classically liberal ethos than freedom of thought and discussion. A cult follower rejects such discussion and, threatened by opposing ideas, replaces discussion with denunciation and "call-outs." Opposition to woke dogmas are deemed hurtful and harmful, and a sign of evil in the other. Fissures in families and old friendships erupt and calcify. This was typified by numerous articles published about friendships and even marriages ending because the woke writer could no longer accept being in relationship with a Trump supporter.

Morally bad behavior is justified for some but intolerable for others

This is perhaps one of the most salient hallmarks of the transition into cult-like behavior. It is not merely that there is moral corruption among adherents, which can and does happen in any group; it is, rather, that the belief in the ideology is the justifying principle that exonerates behavior that otherwise would be deemed repugnant. Looting, vandalism, and violence against cult transgressors is excused or justified when done for the sake of the ideology.

Attacks, shuns, and delegitimizes those who stray from dogma

This is evidenced in cancel culture. To be woke is to see the pervasive evil in every aspect of the world. What deviates from woke doctrine is problematic. Evangelizing happens through shaming.

Harbors persecution complexes and catastrophic thinking

The basis of the ideology is that persecution and oppression are everywhere, even in small and inadvertent ways such as microaggressions, and that such microaggressions are a type of violence. This encourages paranoia and hyper-reactivity.

Sloganeering to avoid serious reflection or questioning

Critical thinking, in the classical liberal tradition, is the activity of the truly free man. Critical theory in the neo-Marxist tradition is the activity of the controlled and controlling man. The beliefs that we arrive at through free and considered analysis we own deeply. If thought is not derived from such internal processes, then it must be imposed externally. Stripped of a meaningful and robust concept of nature, reason, and the human person, woke ideology is a house of cards that requires allegiance through intimidation and power. As Hannah Arendt discovered in observing the trial of Eichmann, the ideologue is characterized by the curious inability to think. Once indoctrinated, thought is replaced by party cliches, propaganda, and sloganeering.

Woke ideology is like a filter sewn onto the mind's eye by which one sifts all knowledge and every human dynamic. It is not unlike a perversion of the C. S. Lewis quote, "I believe in Christianity as I believe that the sun has risen: not only because I see it, but because by it I see everything else." With Christ, we begin to see everything in this world as signs and shadows of his perfect goodness. Through woke ideology, we begin to see everything as signs and shadows of oppression.

10

Education Activism

I n his 1932 book *Toward Soviet America*, William Z. Foster, the national chairman of the American Communist Party, left little doubt of the party's goal for American education. "Among the elementary measures the American Soviet government will adopt to further the cultural revolution are . . . [a] National Department of Education . . . the studies will be revolutionized, being cleansed of religious, patriotic, and other features of the bourgeois ideology. The students will be taught the basis of Marxian dialectical materialism, internationalism and the general ethics of the new Socialist society."[1]

Around the same time, John Dewey, perhaps the most influential figure in modern American education, was facilitating the Frankfurt School's move to Columbia University. Dewey, a socialist and staunch atheist, had made a pilgrimage to Soviet Russia in 1928. Upon his return to the States, he wrote a book of his admiration for, and desire to replicate, the way in which their education system was used as

---

[1]   William Z. Foster, "Toward Soviet America," Marxists.org, accessed November 14, 2020, https://www.marxists.org/archive/foster/1932/toward/06.htm.

a political tool. He harbored an appreciation for how they embedded collectivist mindsets into children and began to dismantle the need for a family unit. "Our special concern here is with the role of the schools in building up forces and factors whose natural effect is to undermine the importance and uniqueness of family life."[2]

Dewey eventually came to be known as the Father of Progressive Education. His understanding of the human person and his disdain for religion animated and informed his view of education. More than an emphasis on reading, writing, and arithmetic, Dewey believed education should be a tool for social engineering and the raising of the consciousness of children toward activism. He taught philosophy of education at the Teacher's College at Columbia where he was able to have a vast and profound impact. By 1950, already a third of principals and superintendents in the country of large school districts had been trained there and returned to their districts to spread Dewey's educational theories throughout the nation.

Marcuse also had a great impact on the future of education through his proximate and ideological influence on the Teacher's College. Additionally, he served as an effective mentor and intellectual hero to the terror group the Weather Underground, whose leaders would later go on to hold influential educational posts. The Weatherman, as it was initially called, was a faction of the radical socialist group (euphemistically named) the Students for Democratic Society (SDS).

---

[2]   John Dewey, *Impressions of Soviet Russia and the Revolutionary World* (Teacher's College: Columbia University, 1964), p. 78.

Like the SDS, the Weather Underground was populated by mostly middle class young adults turned activists. It was this group which was responsible for bombings of the United States Capitol, the Pentagon, and several police stations in New York, as well as the Greenwich Village townhouse explosion that killed three of its members.

After the gruesome Tate and La Bianca murders by followers of Charles Manson, one leader of the Weather Underground, Bernadine Dohrn, notoriously said with glee, "Offing those rich pigs with their own forks and knives, and then eating a meal in the same room, far out! The Weathermen dig Charles Manson." Other quotes from Ms. Dohrn have her marveling that a fork was plunged into the stomach of one victim. The Weather Underground members would often greet one another with fingers stretched apart to indicate a fork as a sign of revolution.[3]

After years on the FBI's ten most wanted list for her violent revolutionary antics, Dohrn went on to have an influential career as a law professor at Northwestern and married fellow former Weather Underground leader Bill Ayers. Also recently retired, Ayers held a tenured and powerful position as distinguished professor of education at the University of Illinois where he trained hundreds of teachers to be activists. Ayers's texts on the imperative of social-justice teaching are still considered among the most popular works in the syllabi of the nation's education schools and teacher-training institutes. "Ayers's politics have hardly changed since his

---

[3] Anthony DeCurtis, "Peace, Love, and Charlie Manson," *The New York Times*, August 1, 2009, https://www.nytimes.com/2009/08/02/weekinreview/02decurtis.html.

Weatherman days," writes education author Sol Stern. "He still boasts about working full-time to bring down American capitalism and imperialism. This time, however, he does it from his tenured perch as Distinguished Professor of Education at the University of Illinois, Chicago."[4]

While he formerly used bombs and violence, in the university setting, Ayers worked more insidiously to indoctrinate future generations of teachers that they might in turn impart the spirit of revolution into their public-school students. "One of Ayers's major themes is that the American public school system is nothing but a reflection of capitalist hegemony. Thus, the mission of all progressive teachers is to take back the classrooms and turn them into laboratories of revolutionary change."[5]

In 2008, Ayers was elected vice president for curriculum of the American Educational Research Association (AERA). The AERA counts twenty-five thousand professors and researchers within its membership and is one of nation's largest organizations of education-school professors and researchers. The goal of the AERA is to transform education from creating critical thinkers to creating critical theorists and activists. In doing so, they know that the education system could become a conveyor belt in the production of new generations of social justice warriors.

---

[4]   Sol Stern, "Obama's Real Bill Ayers Problem," *City Journal*, April 23, 2008, https://www.city-journal.org/html/obama's-real-bill-ayers-problem-10390.html.

[5]   Ibid.

The Education Complex Against the Family

A particular target in the progressive education model is, unsurprisingly, the family. Adorno, in his famous 1950 work *The Authoritarian Personality*, claimed to discover that the traditional American father was actually an oppressive "authoritarian" because he held traditional values. Progressives knew that to immediately attempt to disrupt the family directly would be too much too soon for mid-century Americans, so in the vein of Adorno, they instead relentlessly attacked the "patriarchy" as an indicator and predicter of fascism.

This sentiment was echoed by Chester M. Pierce, a notable professor of education and psychiatry at Harvard and consultant for such children's educational shows as *Sesame Street*. "Every child in America entering school at the age of five is mentally ill because he comes to school with certain allegiances to our Founding Fathers, toward our elected officials, toward his parents, toward a belief in a supernatural being, and toward the sovereignty of this nation as a separate entity," Pierce argued. "It's up to you as teachers to make all these sick children well—by creating the international child of the future."[6]

The public school system, as Dewey had gleaned from his visit to Soviet Russia, had the power to become an effective reeducation mechanism that stressed secular humanist values and the collectivist mindset. The National Education Association (NEA) grew under the thumb of Marxist and communist organizers in its commitment to override the

---

[6]   Speech given at the 1973 International Education Seminar.

influence of parents over their children. Secular humanist activist and Unitarian Universalist minister Charles Francis Potter believed that secular humanism was not the end of religion but the beginning of a new one based on man, not God. Schools, he believed, would become secular seminaries indoctrinating the future. "Education is thus a most powerful ally of humanism, and every public school is a school of humanism." Potter went on, "What can the theistic Sunday school, meeting for an hour once a week, and teaching only a fraction of the children, do to stem the tide of a five-day program of humanistic teachings?"[7]

The revolutionary goal for the early elementary years was to separate children from parents, not only physically, but also by undermining and fracturing the influence and authority of parents by injecting a slow drip of ideology into the school system. Essential to this effort is the introduction of the child, as early as possible, to adult sexual practices. This is done with the goal of removing from his psyche any sense of responsibility or guilt and to build up his "self-esteem" by removing all competitive motivation. Confirming Unwin's findings, the early sexualization and the breakdown of sexual norms ushered in a compromising of rational thought, personal motivation, and cultural achievement.

Mary Calderone, an influential public advocate for the radical sexual education of children, stated her impatience with the time it took for the real goals of education to be fulfilled. "We have yet to beat our drums for birth control in

---

[7]   *AZ Quotes*, s.v. "Charles Francis Potter," accessed November 15, 2020, https://www.azquotes.com/quote/766022.

the way we beat them for polio vaccine. We are still unable to put babies in the class of dangerous epidemics, even though this is the exact truth."[8]

While that was in the 1960s, unfortunately, things have not changed much. In 2019, a new action item was adopted by the NEA:

> The NEA will honor the leadership of women, non-binary, and trans people, and other survivors who have come forward to publicly name their rapists and attackers in the growing, international, #MeToo movement.
>
> Furthermore, the NEA will include an assertion of our defense of a person's right to control their own body, especially for women, youth, and sexually marginalized people. The NEA vigorously opposes all attacks on the right to choose and stands on the fundamental right to abortion under Roe v. Wade.[9]

There can be little doubt about the radical politicization of the education establishment. During the Covid quarantine of 2020, with schools shut down, the Los Angeles teacher's union put out a statement that they would not consider reopening until their demands were met. These demands included such political items as defunding the police, Medicare for all, and a moratorium on funding for charter schools.[10]

---

[8]   Medical Morals newsletter, February-March 1968.

[9]   "New Business Item 56 (2019)," NEA, accessed November 02, 2020, https://ra.nea.org/business-item/2019-nbi-056/.

[10]   https://wearepublicschools.org/wp-content/uploads/2020/07/SameStormDIffBoats_FINAL.pdf. 11/01/20.

There is little daylight left between activists and educators. For the more elite, the distinction is obliterated. In the left journal the *Nation*, the author of *Full Surrogacy Now*, Sophie Lewis, argues that in the wake of the Covid quarantine, new understandings of household arrangements were in demand. Her book, she hoped, "might contribute to a revival of queer utopianism inspired by the Marxist rallying cry 'Abolish the family.'" She is not alone, as she goes on to reference her fellow academics:

> Indeed, for several years now, together with a number of other trans-liberationist Marxists and mothers—notably Michelle O'Brien, Kate Doyle-Griffiths, Madeline Lane-McKinley, and Jules Joanne Gleeson—I have been doing my best to raise the profile again of that old dream "family abolition," to clarify what it is and isn't, and to restore the private (repro-normative or patriarchal) nuclear household to its proper place as the principal object of feminist and queer radical critique. And here, critique really means critique: recognition that the family as we know it is, simultaneously, an anti-queer factory for producing productive workers, rife with power asymmetries and violence, and the sole source of love, care, and protection against the brutalization of the police, the market, work, and racism, many of us have got.[11]

---

[11]   Sophie Lewis, "Covid-19 Is Straining the Concept of the Family. Let's Break It." *The Nation*, June 3, 2020, https://www.thenation.com/article/society/family-covid-care-marriage/.

Evidence that this ideological unanimity has had a large effect on the educational formation of the young is abundant. A few notable findings from a 2019 poll by the Victims of Communism Memorial Foundation reveal that communism is viewed favorably by more than one in three millennials (36 percent). This is an eight point increase from 2018. Just 57 percent of millennials (compared to 94 percent of the silent generation, who came just prior to the boomers) believe the Declaration of Independence better guarantees freedom and inequality over the Communist Manifesto. Compared to the 1 percent of the silent generation, about one in five millennials (22 percent) believe that "society would be better if all private property was abolished."[12]

The historical amnesia about the dangers of communism and socialism is "on full display," said Marion Smith, executive director of the Victims of Communism Memorial Foundation. "When we don't educate our youngest generations about the historical truth of 100 million victims murdered at the hands of communist regimes over the past century, we shouldn't be surprised at their willingness to embrace Marxist ideas."[13]

In 1941, Eugene Lyons wrote *Enemy in our Schools* about the corruption of the educational system and the effort to lace lesson plans with Marxist ideology. In it he explains how college teachers slant their lessons to match the latest views out of Moscow and would meet with the communist leaning

---

[12]   "2019 Annual Poll," Victims of Communism Memorial Foundation, accessed September 21, 2020, https://victimsofcommunism. org/annual-poll/2019-annual-poll/.

[13]   Ibid.

students in "conspiratorial caucuses." Lyons stated that the trend of glorifying the youth was strategic because it "puts a premium on lack of experience, mental fuzziness and intuition as against intelligence and maturity."[14]

It is alarming how, eighty years later, we have the spoils of these ideological investments all around us. The combination of historical ignorance, the early sexualization of children through sex education and media, and the anti-family propaganda campaigns have all been seeded into the very institutions once tasked to impart knowledge, critical thinking, and good judgment. Instead of teaching them *how* to think, we teach students political narratives of *what* to think. In effect, we teach them how to be activists. In doing so, we have encouraged shallow but sharp passions, peevishness, and arrogance. Perhaps worst of all, the educational system has severed generations of youth from the patrimony of the parents who entrusted them to these institutions.

Idea Laundering

How do so many revolutionary ideas and terms become cloaked in academic legitimacy? To explain this phenomenon, biologist and evolutionary theorist Brett Weinstein coined the term "idea laundering." Idea laundering is like money laundering, only rather than baptizing the corruptly obtained money through a shell business, idea laundering baptizes corruptly pre-ordained conclusions through

---

14   Eileen F. Toplansky, "Were Christians Always so Left-Wing?" *American Thinker*, July 26, 2020, https://www.americanthinker.com/articles/2020/07/were_christians_always_so_leftwing.html.

universities. In this climate, an academic ideologue with the right critical theory agenda can confirm almost anything as knowledge if he begins with the preferred political conclusion.

Writing about idea laundering in the *Wall Street Journal*, Peter Boghossian explains that this process begins with academics having strong moral impulses about something. He uses the example of obesity and a desire to stop negative attitudes about it in society. The academics "convince themselves that the clinical concept of obesity (a medical term) is merely a story we tell ourselves about fat (a descriptive term)." Boghossian goes on to say about obesity, "it's not true or false—in this particular case, it's a story that exists within a social power dynamic that unjustly ascribes authority to medical knowledge."[15]

The studies are embarked upon in a seemingly noble effort to resolve a societal ill—fat shaming. In the hypothetical, the sentiments are widely shared and a peer-reviewed journal is established and credentialed academics are tasked with looking over submissions. Articles are published by the journal's founder and contributors. Before long, there is a canon of work establishing the laundered ideas' authenticity and institutional credibility. "Ideas and moral impulses go in, knowledge comes out. . . . Students leave the academy

---

[15]   Peter Boghossian, "'Idea Laundering' in Academia," *The Wall Street Journal*, November 24, 2019, https://www.wsj.com/articles/idea-laundering-in-academia-11574634492?email-Token=a34216fe20106dbb87d89d771b55eb1d210VHy du2YuKbvUpabq08vB2lsLr8JmMnd/DsAlWc55Qfx85rrvxw JWTopEw0Bg1KAdsTgI9+RIaCGWbu5/1dw%3D%3D&re flink=article_copyURL_share.

believing they know things they do not know." Boghossian continues, "They bring this 'knowledge' to their places of employment where, over time, laundered ideas and the terminology that accompanies them become normative—giving them even more unearned legitimacy."[16]

Suppose a student skeptical of the laundered idea pushes back, protesting that while fat-shaming is bad and should be discouraged, there are other correlatives that indicate genuine health risks which have nothing to do with power structures but rather originate in the biology of the human body. With the canon already in place, such students can be directed to a body of peer reviewed articles containing the "correct" answers and the veneer of intellectual inquiry.

Though this is a hypothetical, it illustrates how modern academia catechizes its students into activism. Boghossian knows this process well. Along with James Lyndsay and Helen Pluckrose, he sought to expose the political corruption of education, highlighting their practice of submitting unsubstantiated and absurd papers to respected academic journals that flattered each journal's preordained political values. The success of their hoax was remarkable. The papers posited such things as the dismissal of western astronomy on the basis that it is sexist and imperialist, or a case for physics departments to study feminist astrology, or practice interpretative dance. Their most famous published paper, entitled "Human Reaction to Rape Culture and Queer Performativity at Urban Dog Parks in Portland, Oregon," claimed to be based on observation of canine rape culture at Portland dog

---

16   Ibid.

parks. "Do dogs suffer oppression based upon (perceived) gender?" the paper asked.[17]

Along with idea laundering comes an explosion of new vocabulary meant to reframe the way we think. New terms—cisgender, intersectionality, rape culture, white privilege—gain academic gravitas, then cultural, seemingly out of nowhere. "They've been laundered through the peer-reviewed literature by activist scholars, then widely taught for years, before being brought into the world."[18]

While this is promulgated in academics, it easily bleeds into media and popular consciousness. Academic researcher Zach Goldberg charted on LexisNexis the rise of modern woke neologisms over the last decade. The results were shockingly similar and revealed a sharp, almost vertical uptick in mentions of each woke neologism he tested. Words such as *privilege* and *social justice* skyrocketed in media mentions between the years 2012 and 2015 and continue to rise thereafter. Another researcher, Daivd Rozado, expanded the search to include *microaggressions, systemic racism*, and *oppression* with similarly dramatic results.[19]

---

[17]   Yascha Mounk, "What an Audacious Hoax Reveals About Academia," *The Atlantic*, October 5, 2018, https://www.theatlantic.com/ideas/archive/2018/10/new-sokal-hoax/572212/.   Another of their papers accepted by an academic journal simply rewrote a chapter of Hitler's *Mein Kampf* as a "Feminist Manifesto." (Amanda Borschel-Dan, "Duped academic journal publishers rewrite of 'Mein Kampf' as feminist manifesto," The Time of Israel, October 5, 2018, https://www.timesofisrael.com/duped-academic-journal-publishes-rewrite-of-mein-kampf-as-feminist-manifesto/).

[18]   Peter Boghossian, "'Idea Laundering' in Academia."

[19]   Rod Dreher, "'Idea Laundering,'" *The American Conservative*, November 26, 2019, https://www.theamericanconservative.com/dreher/boghossian-idea-laundering-wokeness-academia/.

Decades of idea laundering have resulted in a canon of scholarship too big to fail. Eventually, we all began to nod along to the terms and conditions of the sophisticated set. We furrow our brow over heteronormativity. We shake our heads disapprovingly about the problem of the patriarchy. This all leads to controlled thought through a corruption of words and the soft coercion of groupthink, tied with a bow of elite, expert approval.

Rewriting History

Part of exerting control over the mind of the nation is through rewiring our cultural memory. Every year, Alexander Riley, a sociology professor at Bucknell University, talks to his students about the 9/11 attacks. While most of them were not yet born on that fateful day, they generally know a few facts about what occurred. But year after year, he discovers the same phenomenon. "When I ask students in the class to describe the single most important lesson learned from 9/11, invariably someone will suggest that it has to do with the extremity of anti-Muslim bias in America. That student will allude to the appalling frequency of hate crimes against American Muslims in the aftermath of the attack." Usually, Riley notes, other students nod their heads in agreement, but never has he had a student challenge this claim despite it being inconsistent with reality. Riley continues, "According to the FBI, hate crimes against Muslims did increase post-9/11. But the annual number of such crimes never reached three figures and has typically stayed well under fifty. At its highest level in 2001, the risk for the average Muslim-American was somewhere around 1 in 31,000."[20]

A glaring and effective example of identity activism rewriting history is the ambitious *1619 Project* launched by the *New York Times* in August 2019. In it, lead writer Nikole Hannah-Jones seeks to reframe the founding of the United States, placing it not with the Declaration of Independence in 1776 but in the year 1619, with the arrival of the first slaves brought by English colonists. Hannah-Jones asserts that America was founded not as a democracy but as a slave-ocracy.

According to this project in the paper of record, all that America is and has, for better or for worse, hinges on the shameful introduction of slavery and the idea that our racist founding permeates the core of every American institution. Racism is, as she claims, in our DNA. Ours is not a country "conceived in liberty, and dedicated to the proposition that all men are created equal," as Abraham Lincoln and the founders understood it to be. To the purveyors of the *1619 Project*, America, rather, is a nation conceived in sin.[21]

Origin stories matter. What binds us as a country is not race but a propositional form of government devoted to inalienable rights and principles, principles which ultimately

---

[20]   Alexander Riley, "Multiculturalism is Ethnocentrism," *The American Mind*, October 9, 2019, https://americanmind.org/essays/multiculturalism-is-ethnocentrism/.

[21]   Nikole Hannah-Jones, "Our democracy's founding ideals were false when they were written. Black Americans have fought to make them true," *The New York Times Magazine*, August 14, 2019, https://www.nytimes.com/interactive/2019/08/14/magazine/black-history-american-democracy.html.

lit the path toward righting the injustice of slavery. This origin story keeps us united and aspiring toward the shared common ideals embedded within it.

Hannah-Jones's most disputed claim is that the American Revolution was fought for the purpose of preserving slavery. Besides the ignorance of history exposed by this account, it is at utter odds with the Declaration itself, which not only says nothing to enshrine slavery but reflects quite deliberately the very principles which would undermine it.

This account is so ahistorical that three esteemed socialist historians, Niles Niemuth, Tom Mackaman, and David North, wrote to dispute it:

> Despite the pretense of establishing the United States' "true" foundation, the 1619 Project is a politically motivated falsification of history. Its aim is to create a historical narrative that legitimizes the effort of the Democratic Party to construct an electoral coalition based on the prioritizing of personal "identities"—i.e., gender, sexual preference, ethnicity, and, above all, race. . . . Hannah-Jones does not view Lincoln as "the Great Emancipator," as the freed slaves called him in the 1860s, but as a garden-variety racist who held "black people [as] the obstacle to national unity." . . . But an honest portrayal of Lincoln would contradict Hannah-Jones' claims that "black Americans fought back alone" to "make America a democracy." So too would a single solitary mention, anywhere in

the magazine, of the 2.2 million Union soldiers who fought and the 365,000 who died to end slavery.[22]

Reframing our understanding of US history into cautionary tales of racism, sexism, patriarchy, and bigotry is necessarily to bias it and circumvent a complex, nuanced comprehensive understanding. History, it seems, is less something to be discovered and more something to be manipulated. Of this, historian Wilfrid McClay says, "Instead of helping us to deepen ourselves and take a mature and complex view of the past, history is increasingly employed as a simple bludgeon, which picks its targets mechanically—often based on little more than a popular cliché—and strikes."[23]

In the 2020 mob vandalism of statuary, there have been all too literal examples of destroying history with a bludgeon. The woke, like the mob, are prone to take a strike not just at historical icons but at our historical record. McClay explains the harm of the *1619 Project*, "If it has any influence, that influence will be as likely as not to damage the nation and distort its self-understanding in truly harmful ways—ways that will perhaps be most harmful of all to Americans of African descent, who do not need to be supplied with yet another reason to feel cut off from the promise of American

---

[22]   Niles Niemuth, Tom Mackaman, and David North, "The New York Times's 1619 Project: A racialist falsification of American and world history," World Socialist Web Site, September 6, 2019, https://www.wsws.org/en/articles/2019/09/06/1619-s06.html.

[23]   Wilfred M. McClay, "The Weaponization of History," *The Wall Street Journal*, August 25, 2019, https://www.wsj.com/articles/the-weaponization-of-history-11566755226?mod=hp_opin_pos_3.

life."[24] McClay acknowledges that slavery was a brutal institution and a contradiction to the nation's highest ideals. But to argue that slavery represents the predominant force shaping the country is a damaging distortion.

Preeminent Civil War scholar James McPherson states that while he approached his reading of the *1619 Project* with eagerness, "almost from the outset, I was disturbed by what seemed like a very unbalanced, one-sided account, which lacked context and perspective on the complexity of slavery, which was clearly, obviously, not an exclusively American institution, but existed throughout history."[25]

In the face of such a preponderance of criticism, Hannah-Jones offered a meager walk-back on her phrasing for clarity, ceding a bit of the ground by admitting that perhaps not every single revolutionary was fighting to preserve slavery.[26] But in true woke fashion, for Hannah-Jones, these scholarly critiques weren't evidence of a misstep on her part so much as indicators of the racist malice on theirs. Hannah-Jones took to Twitter in late 2019 to say of her critics, "Trump supporters have never harassed me and insulted my intelligence as much as white men claiming to be socialists. You all have truly revealed yourselves for the anti-black folks

---

24   Wilfred M. McClay, "How The New York Times Is Distorting American History," *Commentary*, October 2019, https://www.commentarymagazine.com/articles/how-the-new-york-times-is-distorting-american-history/.

25   Rod Dreher, "'Idea Laundering.'"

26   Adam Serwer, "The Fight Over the 1619 Project Is Not About the Facts," *The Atlantic*, December 23, 2019, https://www.theatlantic.com/ideas/archive/2019/12/historians-clash-1619-project/604093/.

you really are."[27] By the summer of the following year, she was more candid about her real aims. "I've always said that the *1619 Project* is not a history. It is a work of journalism that explicitly seeks to challenge the national narrative and, therefore, the national memory. The project has always been as much about the present as it is the past."

Rather than discredited, the *1619 Project* garnered a Pulitzer Prize and is slated to be installed as an educational curriculum in schools across the country. It will likely be understood to be a historical account by students rather than what even the lead author admits it is: an attempt to reimagine our historical memory in service of our political agenda. The opening line of the Pulitzer winning essay from Hannah-Jones begins, "Our democracy's founding ideals were false when they were written."[28] Truly it proves that the concept of idea laundering does not remain in the academy but is present in the corruption of journalism and then fed into the school system where it will be absorbed and regurgitated by new generations back into the culture.

For a country conceived in sin, there is no place, no relationship, no soul not implicated and infected with racism. We can tinker here or there and attend seminars, but the fundamental problem is too pervasive and embedded to be resolved, short of a total transformation of the country. The

---

27   Ida Bae Wells (@nhannahjones), Twitter, accessed November 22, 2020, https://twitter.com/nhannahjones/status/11995254262862 06976.

28   Nikole Hannah-Jones, "Our democracy's founding ideals were false when they were written. Black Americans have fought to make them true."

importance for any totalitarian regime to reshape history in a way that supports and reinforces a conceptual understanding of society which favors the ideological narrative of the regime cannot be overstated.

This tactic of revisionist history attempts to view the past through a sexual lens as well. Benjamin Perry, a pastor and regular contributor to the leftist Christian periodical *Sojourners*, went viral on Twitter in 2020 when he wrote, "Queer communities offer a beautiful lens through which to view the relationship between Jesus and his disciples. The lines between affection, attraction, intimacy and sex are far blurrier than white evangelicals would like them to appear. Let's talk about a bisexual Christ." He went on to say that all theology is sexual and that we have crafted Jesus out of our assumed heterosexual constraints. Then Perry asks, "But what if we cast these assumptions aside? The neat, clean lines between 'heterosexuality' and 'homosexuality' are modern convention. They try to enforce order and discipline on unruly appetites—love and lust." Perry proceeded to speculate blasphemous things about our Lord and his apostles, and then concluded, "Evangelical homophobia clearly violates Christ's teaching, but we less frequently interrogate the host of heteronormative assumptions we ascribe to biblical texts."[29]

For the woke, if there is a sin, it is our perniciously orthodox views on sexuality. The worst sin is to believe that there is such a thing as sin in this arena. Training generations of

---

[29]   Benjamin Perry (@FaithfullyBP), Twitter, April 30, 2020, https://twitter.com/faithfullybp/status/1255849452151148544?s=21.

Americans to reject the stabilizing institutions from family, to church, to the founding principles of our government, to reason itself was never going to end well. In destabilizing them, we have destabilized ourselves. For the woke and their acolytes, at the core of the human person, there is no core. We are no more than a collection of social identities, members in various social groups with no fixed history or origin story to unite us.

PART IV

Restoration

11

The Person

A woke conception of the person is fundamentally at
odds with a Christian one. For the woke, a person can
be defined by asking two questions. The first is "What do I
desire?" By this metric, the good life is identical to the ability
to live out one's desires unencumbered by others, by social
demands, by religion, by government, or even by nature.
Such a vision of the good life does not preclude entering into
marriage or joining a church community or other mutually
cooperative arrangements. It also does not preclude will-
ingly giving up certain desires for the sake of others, such
as when a person diets or trains for a marathon. So long as
such arrangements and disciplines serve the greater goal of
the full expression of the individual's will, such things will
serve us well. But once such entanglements cease to serve
the therapeutic self, they can and should end. Religion, for
example, can serve as a comfort, or a means of self-help, but
it cannot place any moral demands on us beyond that.

There is not much that this view will disavow except perhaps non-consensual activity. Consent is allowed as the thin
dividing line between the moral and immoral because it is
the line at which the will of one person pushes against the

will of another. Nothing is intrinsically wrong unless a participant objects to it. This leads to all sorts of absurdities. For example, we are to believe that sex is so meaningless that we can engage in it with whomever we want but simultaneously see it as so personal that an unsolicited hug can be considered sexual assault. When nothing is wrong, anything can be offensive.

The second question that the woke use to define a person is "How have I been hurt?" The first question, rooted in the therapeutic, leads to the second question, rooted in grievance. Both locate the person on an axis of power—how it can be attained and how it can be denied.

In contrast, a Christian understanding of the human person is not that he is a will seeking power but rather that he is beloved by God, made in his image, and therefore has obligations to him and to others. Author and scholar Carter Snead says that we can look to how we enter the world to learn something about our nature and purpose. "I come into the world not as a radical isolated will that can pursue its own projects, but as a baby. There's something about the anthropological realities of newborns that teach us something really important about who we are fundamentally."[1] Human beings need one another. Any woman experiencing pregnancy and postpartum knows it is harrowing stuff to go it alone. A child without a father or a mother intuitively knows the depth of that void. We are vulnerable, and our

---

[1]   Carter Snead, "Carter Snead Explains the Secular Vs. Catholic View of the Human Person," YouTube video posted by Magis Center, July 3, 2020, https://www.youtube.com/watch?v=_PpF 4dVdwJs.

need for one another also signifies that we have duties to one another.

The Christian conception of the person considers that our bodies, as integral parts of our being, reveal and prescribe truths about who we are and what we ought to do. These are truths which are independent of what we might desire at any given time but are intimately tied to what will bring about our happiness—not a happiness that is located in hopscotching from pleasure to pleasure as though that were our end but rather a happiness in coming to live in harmony with the reality of our nature as rational and embodied beings.

Self-knowledge

The extreme emphasis on self-expression today is a reflection of a desire to be known and loved. It is a right desire that, once stripped from its true source, becomes manifest in disordered ways. To really know ourselves is not just to know what we want but to be able and willing to evaluate it in light of an objective understanding of the good. Flannery O'Connor said succinctly, "To know oneself is, above all, to know what one lacks. It is to measure oneself against Truth, and not the other way around. The first product of self-knowledge is humility."[2]

Similarly, self-knowledge is also made difficult when we are absorbed into groups bound by mutual grievances. This sort of identity tribalism magnifies our perception of the ills of others and hinders our ability to see the deficits in

---

[2]   Flannery O'Connor, *Mystery and Manners: Occasional Prose* (New York: Farrar, Straus, and Giroux, 1957).

ourselves. As Girard's mimetic theory indicates, it is easy to be pulled into a grievance identity no matter what our politics. Conservatives can relish together their hatred of liberals, women can bond over their frustrations with their husbands, as can men scapegoat women. No one is above this tendency, underscoring why we are in dire need of the self-knowledge that comes with self-examination.

Such grievance groups have a scientifically supported contagion effect with respect to bad behavior. For example, researchers from Brown University, Harvard University, and the University of California at San Diego found that a person is 75 percent more likely to become divorced if a friend has divorced.[3]

While this can seem merely correlative, evidence and common sense point to a causal connection, with results of their study suggesting that divorce can spread between friends. "Clusters of divorces extend to two degrees of separation in the network. . . . Overall, the results suggest that attending to the health of one's friends' marriages may serve to support and enhance the durability of one's own relationship, and that, from a policy perspective, divorce should be understood as a collective phenomenon that extends beyond those directly affected."[4]

An essential weapon against the pull into grievance bonding is through self-examination and self-knowledge. So

---

[3]   Rose McDermott, James H. Fowler, and Nicholas A. Christakis, "Breaking Up is Hard to Do, Unless Everyone Else is Doing it Too: Social Network Effects on Divorce in a Longitudinal Sample," *Social Forces*, vol. 92, no. 2, October 8, 2013.

[4]   Ibid.

important is this that without it, our faith is rootless. St. John Henry Newman writes, "Without self-knowledge you have no root in yourselves personally; you may endure for a time, but under affliction or persecution your faith will not last. This is why many in this age (and in every age) become infidels, heretics, schismatics, disloyal despisers of the Church. They cast off the form of truth because it never has been to them more than a form. They do not endure, because they never have tasted that the Lord is gracious; and they never have had experience of His power and love, because they have never known their own weakness and need."[5]

Authentic wholeness can never be sought through the deconstruction of the person down to her desires and grievances. Under the guise of the therapeutic, we have introduced something that is horrifically anti-therapeutic. If we do not understand who God is, we will never understand who we are. Correspondingly, a fundamental lie in our anthropology obscures and deforms our theology.

Collectivizing Sin

Around the turn of the last century, Protestant theologian Walter Rauschenbusch attempted to merge the city of man and the city of God by fusing his Christian faith with the burgeoning socialism movement. Rauschenbusch argued that Christians needed to understand sin less as an individual matter and instead as a social one. Evil, he claimed, is located in socio-economic and political institutions, what he called "suprapersonal entities": militarism, individualism,

---

[5]   John Henry Newman, Sermon: "Parochial and Plain."

capitalism, and nationalism. Against these, Rauschenbusch juxtaposed four institutional embodiments of good: pacifism, collectivism, socialism, and internationalism.[6]

Author Joseph Bottum identifies Rauschenbusch's influence, among others, as popularizing the social gospel in a way that would have far-reaching effects on American pieties. By socializing sin and making it abstract, the social gospel movement stripped Christians of their felt need for Christ.

The problem Bottum identifies is that a social gospel tends to reduce Christianity to a social club. Christ is reduced to the means of the more pressing goal of social justice. "Christ is the ladder by which we climb to the new ledge of understanding, but once we're on that ledge, we don't need the ladder anymore." [7]

Bottum posits that we are in a post-Protestant culture, but that our spiritual anxieties persist, leading us to adopt social justice with the spiritual fervor left behind from lingering attachments to the Christianity that we have largely abandoned.

If the transformation of the Christian landscape is owed in part to the abandonment of contending with our personal sin, a remedy is to face it squarely again. One of the hardest things to do is honestly assess our own situation. The temptation toward thinking that we are better off than

---

[6] Walter Rauschenbusch, *A Theology for the Social Gospel* (New York: Abingdon Press, 1917).

[7] Mark Tooley and Joseph Bottum, "America amid Spiritual Anxiety: A Conversation with Joseph Bottum," *Providence*, June 19, 2020, https://providencemag.com/video/america-amid-spiritual-anxiety-a-conversation-with-joseph-bottum/.

we actually are is one of our biggest hurdles to improvement. We are experts at self-deception. It is certainly easier to believe that I'm ok and you're ok. Truth is difficult to tell and hard to hear. We instinctively recoil at being corrected. We need a firm commitment to sincerity—to freedom from deceit, duplicity, and hypocrisy—knowing that we will not achieve it with perfection in this life.

In ancient Rome, skilled sculpture artists were in high demand but low in supply, creating a market for less skilled artists who would patch through their work with wax to cover their imperfections. The word *sincerity* means "seen wax." A trained eye was one that could see the wax and not be fooled by it, indicating that sincerity is a sort of skill for which we train. The ability to train our eyes to see our faults is necessary if we are to see our need. Sincerity with self is the runway to self-improvement. Sincerity with others is the road to true relationships.

In Alcoholics Anonymous, each member must start her participation in every meeting by announcing that she is an alcoholic. At Weight Watchers, every member must weigh in and face his situation with clarity. As Catholics, it is essential to speak our sins to Christ through the priest *in persona Christi* that we might develop habits of examining our consciences, confessing our sins, receiving sacramental grace, resolving to improve, and receiving the real grace of the sacrament of Penance. Such habits alert us to our vanities and ego and in turn inspire in us reverence and humility.

Clinical psychologist and popular author Jordan Peterson speaks to the challenges and importance of habitual examination of conscience on a natural level:

One thing you do if you're a sensible person is you kind of view your own positive motivations with a bit of skepticism. . . . It's always worth giving some consideration for whether there's some darker motives beneath your so-called saintly goodness. Saintly goodness actually is in rather short supply so if you're laying out a claim to that you better be sure you're right. You better be sure you've examined your conscience. . . . People tend not to do that because it's a rather dismal affair examining your conscience and you tend to find out that there are a number of rather dark things going on under the surface that you'd rather not admit.[8]

If the tendency toward defining ourselves based on grievances is the road to despair and the bifurcation of the person, sincerity and self-examination are the hopeful and foundational means to restoring ourselves.

Made for Redemption

Without firmly facing our sins, we lose the ability to combat them and the possibility of redemption. And while we need to avail ourselves of natural remedies as well, the Church, in her wisdom, sets us on a path that also unites natural aid within supernatural grace.

Jack Bingham is a Catholic convert who writes about the demons and addictions he has battled already at a young age, the misery that accompanied them, and the freedom he

---

8   Jordan Peterson, "Identity Politics & The Marxist Lie of White Privilege," YouTube video posted by Sovereign Nations, January 30, 2018, https://www.youtube.com/watch?v=ofmuCXRMoSA.

found through the sacrament of confession. "Catholicism has given me what drugs, alcohol, sex, and porn promised me." He goes on to say this sacrament has been integral in helping him to break habitual sin. "Early in my journey when tempted by sin I literally had thoughts like 'I don't want to do this cause then I'll have to go to confession.' It bred a sense of accountability I couldn't achieve on my own."[9]

There's a powerful scene in the television show *Breaking Bad* during a Narcotics Anonymous meeting at which Jesse Pinkman, plagued with guilt over having murdered a man (but unable to admit it), "confesses" to having heartlessly killed a dog instead. When one woman in the group expresses shock and disgust, she is quickly quieted by the group leader and told not to judge. The leader's words, while well-meaning, are abrasively inadequate in the face of Jesse's sorrow. Jesse responds, "If you just do stuff and nothing happens, what's it all mean? What's the point? Oh right, this whole thing is just about self-acceptance? . . . So, I should stop judging and accept? So no matter what I do, hooray for me because I'm a great guy?"[10]

We are a culture absorbed in self-acceptance. But human nature being what it is, we are also a people immersed in guilt. We betray, we use other people, we tell lies to ourselves and to others, we are selfish and egotistical. Without a common vocabulary to put this guilt in its proper context, our

---

9   Jack A. Bingham (@HopeCatholic), Twitter, https://twitter.com/HopeCatholic.

10   *Breaking Bad*, Ep. "Problem Dog."

only recourse is to deny that it's there, even while sensing that something is still amiss.

This tends to make us recoil when others state obvious truths. There's nothing more offensive than hearing the truth we are trying to silence in ourselves. We think it is better to become the accuser, the one who judges nothing but is contemptuous of everything. Confronted with his despair, Pinkman sensed that if there is to be a way out, it isn't the thin compassion of generic self-acceptance, a tin can in the face of a flood.

In giving a sacramental architecture to our spiritual life, the Church gives us the opportunity and obligation to routinely examine the state of our souls and see ourselves honestly, as well as regularly experience a real and profound encounter with forgiveness. When sincerely done, the sacrament of confession prompts us to confront our weaknesses and failures in a way that disposes us to look more mercifully on one another and to know of our profound need for a merciful God.

Being Known by Others

The depersonalization of the culture and the rise of social media has created a uniquely modern experience of being able to see vast amounts of people who do not see us back, much less know us. This is acutely exhibited in celebrity culture and our democratization of it through social media, which brings celebrity within the grasp of everyone. Being seen has become irresistible. But being seen and being known are different things.

The modern person tends to be fractured—consumed with projecting who he wants to be and concealing who he is, all the while hoping the projection is the reality. But the possibility that the projection is not real—that he cannot be known because he cannot face himself—gnaws at him.

This fracturing is why we have become so preoccupied with convincing ourselves that we are worthy of esteem. We tell ourselves that we are beautiful and strong and powerful, but what if we are sometimes mean and weak-willed? We begin to see it but then distract, affirm, and squint away from it.

So desperate are we to elevate our preferred view of self over reality that we turn away from the other or see the other as a means for affirming our projected selves. We remain bifurcated, fractured, seen but not known. Divided and weak, we justify our actions even when we suspect they might be gravely and morally wrong; then we ask (demand) others to justify them as well.

In contrast, intimacy with another is terrible and beautiful; it forces us to both see ourselves and get outside of ourselves. We can't love what we don't know. There is a particularity and a vulnerability to love. The things we wish were not there cannot be wished away when someone else really knows us. We become people who think with reality in a way that is both humbling and hopeful.

In concert with growing in self-knowledge comes this intimate friendship with others. A new sincerity blossoms that allows another to truly know us, and in return, we see ourselves with clarity. Avoiding such honesty in friendship can be a consequence of avoiding God, whose face we will only behold one day if we are in sincere friendship with him in this life. Whether or not we know him, he knows us more deeply than we know ourselves . . . and that is a terrible and beautiful thing to face.

Knowing ourselves with clarity helps us to see others with generosity. Many are experiencing the sting of division in our friendships and families over the turmoil of 2020. It is good to remember that persons are not identical to movements. Though we might be tempted to post bile on social media, or react to the bile of others, it's helpful to remember most people are less consumed by ideology than these limited platforms might indicate. If this is all we are seeing of each, it becomes easy to dehumanize and depersonalize the other.

The reality is that though some do become militant expressions of wokeness, most have just absorbed it through the ambient messaging that pervades institutions shaping our culture. From the education system to major media outlets, from pop culture to Madison Avenue, we are given a filter through which we see most everything without realizing we are looking through a filter at all. It can help to see our contemporaries as having fallen prey to ideology rather than being the drivers of it. They are receptors of the poison drip, not the administrators.

Everyone is susceptible to growing contemptuous of friends and family, especially when the stakes are high and the consequences are deeply felt. Hatred for an ideology can easily become hatred for the person espousing it, and this would be the true triumph of the very thing we think we are fighting. Dorothy Day summed up the radical call to love, "I really only love God as much as the person I love the least."

An essential element of friendship is the ability to move beyond seeing the superficial aspects of the other—this person is overweight, this person is strikingly good-looking, this person is very old and wrinkly, this person is a different race. We still see those things in a literal sense, but there is a real way in which we see beyond these attributes. The person just becomes Nicholas or Sarah, Irene or Phillip.

This natural movement into the intimacy of friendship has become problematic for the woke. Colorblindness is now considered naïve at best, if not further evidence of racism. Skin color, to the woke, is not a superficial attribute; it is at the core of the human person. To stop seeing color is to stop seeing who someone really is. According to author Ibram X. Kendi, "The common idea of claiming 'color blindness' is akin to the notion of being 'not racist'—as with the 'not racist,' the color-blind individual, by ostensibly failing to see race, fails to see racism and falls into racist passivity. The language of color blindness—like the language of 'not racist'—is a mask to hide racism."[11]

Declaring color blindness to be problematic is effectively to say that true friendship is not only impossible but oppressive. The fundamental goal of human relationship in this model is not friendship but the infernal emphasis on division. This ideology is an obstacle to friendship and to love in general by encouraging the continual scanning for

---

[11]   Ibram X. Kendi, *How to Be an Antiracist* (Random House) Kindle Edition, p. 10.

transgressions to expose for the sake of validating our essential nature as the oppressed.

The disposition of the saint animated by the love of Christ is radically different. St. Thérèse described how she would increase in love for her neighbor, especially when the devil would put before her an over-awareness of another's faults, by instead seeking out her virtues. "I tell myself that if I have seen her fall one time, she may well have undergone a great many victories that she hides through humility. . . . Ah, I understand now that perfect charity consists of enduring the faults of others, of not being at all astonished at their weaknesses, of being edified by the smallest acts of virtue which one sees them practice."[12] It is so easy to see another's faults, and we quickly ascribe evil motives to them. This is the necessary ritual of the woke ideology. But it is the death of love.

Christ modeled a different way. "No longer do I call you servants, for the servant does not know what his master is doing; but I have called you friends, for all that I have heard from my Father I have made known to you" (Jn 15:15). He brings us into divine filiation, which in turn allows us to be in profound familial relationship with one another. It is through him that we are encouraged to think with reality, to see things as they are, to know both our existential poverty and our supernatural calling. Our fundamental struggle is not with a system but with ourselves. Through this struggle, we begin to decrease so that he might increase in us.

A newspaper columnist once put out a query to famous authors to answer the question "What is wrong with the

---

12   St. Thérèse of Lisieux, *Story of A Soul* (TAN Books), Chapter IX.

world today?" A reply came in from one particularly elegant
and pithy writer:

> Dear Sir,
> What is wrong with the world?
> I am.
> Yours sincerely,
> G. K. Chesterton

The Family

The remedy for the error of elevating groups over persons is not to deny our need for group belonging. The remedy is to discern the sort of group that respects, rather than diminishes, the personhood of the individual.

Persons are meant to exist in groups. An extreme individualism which dismisses the need for one to be in community will not serve as a proper antidote to the tribalism of identity politics. Rather than seeing community and the individual as opposed to each other, Dietrich von Hildebrand points to the harmony that ought to exist between them. He writes, "[The person and the community] are so linked that it is impossible to do real justice to the real nature of the person or the community whenever one is emphasized at the expense of the other. If we lose sight of their deep interrelationship we necessarily blind ourselves even to the nature and rank of the one that is overstressed."[1] When we are in communion with others, we become fully ourselves. The foundational community from which society and culture flow is one that, by nature (if not perfectly in practice),

---

[1]   Dietrich von Hildebrand, *Trojan Horse in the City of God* (Sophia Institute Press, 1993), p. 21.

values each individual member as unique and irreplaceable. It is the family.

Family Privilege

Family members appropriately privilege each other, not out of prejudice, but out of duty and the natural bonds of affection. John Seita, author of *Kids Who Outwit Adults,* writes that family privilege is a form of human capital that compounds its benefits over time. Today, however, large numbers of youth go through their lives without the support of stable parents or an extended family. "Even in traditional families," Seita writes, "Family Privilege is not a given. It must be intentional, not simply hit or miss or hope and pray. Those of us with Family Privilege take it for granted. Like oxygen, we would never notice its absence unless we were suffocating."[2]

Family privilege is something each human deserves and is a duty incumbent on every parent. It conveys a natural and good order to human persons and a harmony that finds the common good of the whole as bound up with the good of the individuals. Parents learn responsibility and the generosity of sacrificial love. Children gain belonging, significance, and safety.

In light of this, it seems surprising that this idea of family privilege is often used pejoratively. The woke connect it to the word *privilege* used more generally, conveying with it a

---

[2]   John R. Seita, "Growing Up Without Family Privilege," *Reclaiming Children and Youth,* vol. 10, no. 3, fall 2001, http://reclaiming-journal.com/sites/default/files/journal-article-pdfs/10_3_Seita.pdf.

dynamic of power, guilt, and oppression. Seita echoes this, "Those who thoughtfully examine their own Family Privilege may come to some disquieting conclusions. Perhaps their accomplishments are as much a product of unearned privileges and circumstances as of individual effort and capacity. Even goals and dreams may be the result of Family Privilege."[3] For an argument against individualism, this is a surprisingly myopic, merit-based view of life. To admit that one might have achieved good things in life in part due to the aid of others most beholden to them is to say that human beings are doing something right. To bestow unearned gifts to its members is at the core of the constitution of the human family. A baby is given to her parents in a state of utter need for care and with no meritorious action available to earn it. If family privilege is problematic, then the family is problematic.

The family is a testament to the inherent dignity of the person. It is a basic and potent prompt to see the gratuitous love of God. While this is worth reflecting on in order to inculcate gratitude and compassion within each person, it bears no analogous lesson with white privilege. Instead, we should be striving to support this privilege for everyone.

Far from a sign of something amiss in society, family members privileging one another is a sign of health. While we should be concerned about the well-being of all people, still our duties are particular, not abstract. If I am sick, it is my husband, not a man across town, who tends to me. It falls within my particular sphere of responsibility to know

---

3   Ibid.

that my child has asthma, or an allergy, or is prone to nightmares. The effort to globalize and collectivize sin and love is really an effort to reject the duties inherent in both. While it sounds nice to think we can change the world, the world is changed through the granular. Loving humanity demands little. Loving the person in front of me demands a lot.

In the pattern of woke ideology, under the pretense of sparing the feelings of the one who doesn't have a particular good, we deny that there is a good to be had at all. Demanding that all family structures be considered equal effectively empties the meaning of family altogether.

If there is noxious privilege here, it is the degree of privilege required to disregard the institution most equipped to improve the lives of people in poverty. A 2014 study from Harvard indicated that the number one predictor of economic mobility for poor children in America is the share of two-parent families in their community.[4] Recent research conducted by the Urban Institute and the Brookings Institution suggests that the increase in child poverty between the 1970s and the 1990s was a direct result of the decline of stable marriages.[5] The Heritage Foundation's Robert Rector summed it up perfectly when he said, "Marriage remains America's strongest anti-poverty weapon."[6]

---

[4]   W. Bradford Wilcox, "Family Matters," *Slate*, January 22, 2014, https://slate.com/human-interest/2014/01/new-harvard-study-where-is-the-land-of-opportunity-finds-single-parents-are-the-key-link-to-economic-opportunity.html.

[5]   Zachary J. McDade, ""Is marriage a solution to income inequality?" *Urban Wire* (blog), October 29, 2014, https://www.urban.org/urban-wire/marriage-solution-income-inequality.

[6]   Robert Rector, "Marriage: America's Greatest Weapon Against

Given the wide and deep benefits of family stability, it should have been easy to anticipate the transformative implications of devaluing it. Like critics who advocate for the demise of capitalism while taking daily advantage of the innumerable advantages conferred upon them through it, those who advocate for the disruption of traditional family structures often do so from the privileged place of being the beneficiaries, even tangentially, of the very thing they seek to discredit.

Father Figures and the True Empowerment of the Person

Stories of people who escaped a cycle of extreme poverty or disfunction tend to have a common theme: someone helped them see themselves as moral agents in charge of their own path rather than letting them get caught up in blaming a system or circumstance for their problems. If family life is tragically not provided in full, the closest remedy is this sort of pivotal person conveying this pivotal message—a message which grievance culture seeks to silence. Telling swaths of people that they are both victims and gods leads to people who can only feel despair and license. It is like administering chemotherapy for the flu. The message makes us sicker and does nothing for the underlying issue. It is difficult to triumph in life if there's no point in rallying to reach an impossible goal.

Child Poverty," The Heritage Foundation, September 16, 2010, https://www.heritage.org/poverty-and-inequality/report/marriage-americas-greatest-weapon-against-child-poverty-0.

In the documentary of his life, *Created Equal*, Supreme Court Justice Clarence Thomas reflects on his poverty-stricken childhood in a broken family. At a young age, his grandparents took him and his brother in. Their grandfather's influence dramatically shifted the trajectories of both their lives. The boys knew at a young age that they were living by their grandfather's good graces and that they had an obligation to triumph over their circumstances. Thomas recounts his grandfather telling him that racism would incline people to underestimate him. Getting angry about that might be justified, but far more powerful would be focusing on what was within his control. His grandfather's advice was for the boys to not give others any room to dismiss them. Get a 100 on a test, his grandfather would say, not a 95. Though illiterate himself, he was determined to form his grandsons well through high expectations, good manners, and personal responsibility. His grandfather was fond of repeating moral maxims time and again, "Old Man Can't is dead—I helped bury him," or "Any job worth doing is worth doing right," or "Waste not, want not," or "Play the hand you're dealt." According to writer Myron Magnet, such simple but forceful expressions of wisdom were for Thomas "a laudable call to face reality and cope with it head-on, without self-pity or bitterness."[7]

Thomas also speaks of his young adulthood dance with 1960s Marxism and how he was perpetually consumed with anger. When Thomas gave himself over to rioting and hatred

---

[7] Myron Magnet, "The Founders' Grandson, Part I," *City Journal*, Autumn 2017, https://www.city-journal.org/html/founders-grandson-part-i-15501.html. Access date 11/28/20.

in reaction to the assassination of Martin Luther King Jr., as well as to resentments over personal, painful experiences with racism, it was the tug of his conscience by his grandfather's teachings, as well as the beckoning of his Catholic formation, that pulled him back from what he knew was a destructive path. After a long night of rioting and mayhem, Thomas stumbled into a Catholic Church, knelt down, and asked God to remove the anger from his heart.

In reflecting back decades later, Thomas writes that his grandfather had never been able to understand how Thomas, a college student, could consider himself oppressed. "He didn't think of himself that way and didn't see why I should. Besides, I had a better hand than he'd ever held—and we both knew it. My life was full of opportunities of which he had never dared to dream." Thomas knew his anger about "the man" was merely a way to avoid his responsibilities. "I'd been drunk on revolutionary rhetoric, but now I knew it was nothing more than talk."[8]

Family Mission

Too close to our own time to see things objectively, we can tend to fall into the grooves of old battle lines and reach back to fight them. C. S. Lewis describes this in *The Screwtape Letters*: "We direct the fashionable outcry of each generation against those vices of which it is least in danger and fix its approval on the virtue nearest to that vice which we are trying to make endemic. . . . The game is to have them

---

[8]   Clarence Thomas, *My Grandfather's Son: A Memoir* (Harper Perennial, 2008).

all running about with fire extinguishers whenever there is a flood, and all crowding to that side of the boat which is already nearly gunwale under. Thus we make it fashionable to expose the dangers of enthusiasm at the very moment when they are all really becoming worldly and lukewarm."⁹ One of the most fashionable societal sins we decry is the patriarchy. But while it can be true that there are bad men and distorted examples of fatherhood, are we grabbing fire extinguishers while confronted with a flood?

The revolution has sought doggedly to encourage the worst behavior in men and then bemoans the state of manhood. What is obscured in all this is what fatherhood is meant to be. "A nation of lost and fatherless boys and drifting young men is terrified that we have too much patriarchy," Anthony Esolen writes. "Why, it reinforces my belief in the existence of demons: unassisted man could never be so blank and stupid as to fear that fathers have too much authority when boys and girls by tens of millions grow up with none at all. Only Beelzebub can explain it."¹⁰

In response to this conundrum, sports commentator Marcellus Wiley used his platform to speak to what family formation means to him. The context was a discussion of the NBA's decision to paint "Black Lives Matter" on basketball courts. Wiley spoke to his cohosts and their audience, "I'm a black man who has been black and my life has mattered since 1974. And this organization was founded in 2013 and

⁹   C. S. Lewis, *The Screwtape Letters*, Letter XXV.

¹⁰   Anthony Esolen, "We Need More Patriarchy, Not Less," *Crisis*, July 15, 2020, https://www.crisismagazine.com/2020/we-need-more-patriarchy-not-less.

I'm proud of you but I've been fighting this fight for me and for others a lot longer." His tone was light but emphatic. "Two things: my family structure is so vitally important to me. Not only the one I grew up in but the one I am trying to create right now. Being a father and a husband, that's my mission in life right now."[11] Wiley said this beaming with pride and purpose. He then asked how he can reconcile his life's mission with the BLM mission statement calling for activists to dismantle the patriarchal practice and disrupt the Western-prescribed nuclear family.

We have a difficult time in the twenty-first century seeing the importance of fatherhood because our vision of it has been obscured either by inadequate examples and harmful embodiments or by the agenda-driven repetition and magnification of old tropes about men, prompting a sort of contempt in women and a sense of aimlessness in men. Wiley's comments went viral because they were so plainly true and presented with winning simplicity. There is no right-thinking woman or child who does not want a strong husband and loving father who approaches his family with joy and purpose.

That we diminish and decry this role while turning a blind eye to its importance is not a man problem, it is a human problem, one which affects us all and for which we

---

[11]   Ian Schwartz, "Marcellus Wiley: NBA's Plan To Paint 'Black Lives Matter' On Basketball Courst Is a Bad Idea, Look At The Statistics," *RealClear Politics*, July 2, 2020, https://www.realclear politics.com/video/2020/07/02/marcellus_wiley_nbas_plan_to_paint_black_lives_matter_on_basketball_courts_is_a_bad_idea_look_at_the_statistics.html.

all bear responsibility. Pope Benedict XVI wrote, "The crisis of fatherhood that we are experiencing today is a basic aspect of the crisis that threatens mankind as a whole."[12]

Statistics show far fewer young adults are marrying than previous generations. Whether that is out of fear or disregard for marriage, it bodes poorly. What can we do to reverse these trends? Like most anything, it begins with doing it well ourselves. Beyond that, we need to push back against the narrative that career is more important (for either spouse) and reinstitute the vision of the family as the preeminent work of life and the avenue to our sanctification.

Much of the conversation surrounding the importance of the family and marriage is couched with caution about roles and subjugation, or worry of limiting or losing ourselves. Each of those fears may be born out in any family, and the Faith is not a panacea for them. But our caution should serve as a prompt for us to treat it with more seriousness rather than indifference or the paralysis of indecision. It should be entered into with prudence, not perfectionism, for such a standard will never be met. Embedded in our fear of doing it poorly is our desire to do it well. That family is abidingly important is a truth plain to anyone not blinded by ideology, and like so many truths of nature, it is one reinforced by reason and affirmed by experience. The litany of attacks against the family are in part because of the power of its truth and the desperate desire to distract from it.

---

[12]   Joseph Ratzinger, *The God of Jesus Christ: Meditations on the Triune God* (San Francisco: Ignatius Press, 2008).

The Christian Family

In his prescient 1933 essay "The Patriarchal Family in History," Christopher Dawson lays out a case for the unique call of the Christian family. It was this new conception of family life which owes much to its patriarchal forebearers, but still finds itself to be distinctive and transformative.

First, he begins by arguing that the human family is the cradle of society. The modern notion that we can get back to a state of utopian nature without sexual restraint is not born out by historical anthropology. Ordering sexuality has always existed to some degree as a way of synthesizing the biological realities presented to us. "This synthesis differs from anything that exists in the animal world in that it no longer leaves man free to follow his own sexual instincts; he is forced to conform them to a certain social pattern."[13] A matrilineal society structured a flow of lineage through the mother's line with the biological father's connection as negligible or non-existent. The patrilineal line is the more consistent and historical structure that connected men to their families. Without access to the direct biological bond that mothers experience, the father was aided by the culture that emphasized the fatherly bond.

Christianity built upon and transformed this notion of the family in two ways. "While the patriarchal family in its original form was an aristocratic institution which was the

---

[13]   Christopher Dawson, "The Patriarchal Family in History," in *Dynamics of World History* (Sheed & Ward, 1956), https://www. catholicculture.org/culture/library/view.cfm?recnum=860.

privilege of a ruling race or a patrician class, the Christian family was common to every class, even to the slaves."[14]

The introduction of the Christian concept of family was first of all a broadening of itself beyond class or status. In commenting on this, author R. V. Young writes, "It is the genius of the Church to be catholic; that is, universal."[15] In this way, the family became more socially egalitarian.

Beside this broadening of marriage socially, the Church also transformed it by insisting on the mutual and bilateral character of sexual obligations. As exclusively as the wife belonged to the husband, so would the husband belong to the wife. In contrast to the pre-Christian marriage, this rendered marriage a more individual and personal relationship as well as more egalitarian spiritually.

Still, it was the order and structure of its traditional formation with its norms of exclusivity and permanence which rendered it able to further cultural advancement. What Dawson gleaned was that though it can be done imperfectly or even poorly, from an anthropological perspective, it serves as one of the best and most effective ways to safeguard civilization.

In striking at marriage and the family structure, woke ideology ultimately strikes at Christ himself. Each of the three distorted dogmas of the woke—diminution of the person, rejection of reason, and contempt of authority—is restored through the engine of a healthy family. Firstly, the family is

---

14   Ibid.

15   R. V. Young, "In Defense of Patriarchy," *The Imaginative Conservative*, August 9, 2020, https://theimaginativeconservative. org/2020/08/in-defense-of-patriarchy-rv-young.html.

deeply personal. Secondly, it fosters order and reason through the transmission of virtue necessary for the well-functioning of the micro society that is family life. Thirdly, the family introduces its members to rightful authority, not through control or domination, but with the care and wisdom to maintain boundaries and nurture a love for the good. It is an authority undergirded by the trust and love that deep affection engenders.

Marriage requires human beings to be in conflict with the part of themselves which is more animalistic, and in its permanence, it provides them with a hedge of protection against whim and impulse. By encouraging fidelity and indissolubility, marriage also addresses the importance of stability for their offspring. Far from the Marxist view that sees the family as an oppressive patriarchal system, it is instead the one best able to account for the needs of all involved. Rather than an institution that leads by necessity to men dominating women, it is set up by its nature for humans to dominate the baser parts of themselves so that they might be better equipped to further the culture. But it is not merely preventative of social ills, it is transfiguring— making its members into something new and generative, a sum greater than its parts.

In contrast, woke ideology strikes at the heart not only of marriage and family but of Christ and his Church. Bishop Sheen powerfully states, "The modern world, which denies personal guilt and admits only social crimes, which has no place for personal repentance but only public reforms, has divorced Christ from His Cross; the Bridegroom and Bride have been pulled apart." Separated from one another, each loses its meaning. "Each has awaited new partners who will pick them up in a kind of second and adulterous union. Communism comes along and picks up the meaningless Cross; Western post-Christian civilization chooses the unscarred Christ."[16] In this divorce, we are left with a broken family and the emptiness of nihilism. The cross without Christ is merciless severity. Embracing Christ without his cross is flaccid sentimentalism.

Author Thomas Howard wrote of the mysterious and somewhat confounding way in which the Faith takes hold of this model of the unity of bridegroom and bride and allows it to be the vehicle by which we discover a host of deeper spiritual realities:

> The computer can, of course, tell us who worked at which task for how many hours yesterday, and therefore whose turn it is today. But it cannot tell us why a man should leave his father and mother and cleave to his wife, nor why that man should push that plow year after year, nor why his wife should stagger about for nine months every couple years bearing the fruit of his momentary pleasure, nor why she should get up a hundred nights in a row to suckle his infant and hers; nor why this ridiculous treadmill is spoken of in a holy Book as being a picture of the mystery of Christ and the Church.
>
> The computer and its programmers will smell a plot and set about to rip it all up. They will demolish the sanctuary and tear down the veils that hide the holy

---

16   Fulton Sheen, *Life of Christ* (Image Books, 1990).

things. But there will be some people who will want to get on with the rite on the belief that it does in fact have something to do with self-giving, which has something to do with Charity, which has something to do with Joy.[17]

Howard sensed the modern approach to this very ordinary domestic path was to approach it like a contract or a computer, stripped of mystery and crying out for reformers to bring their calculations of equity and take their wrench to it. But without understanding the profound spiritual truths embedded in this simple structure, we risk misdiagnosing the entire enterprise. In the traditional family formation, we find a metaphor for our communion with the divine. Additionally, Dawson saw the Christian family as analogous to the relationship between the Old and New Testaments. "The former is fulfilled and spiritually transfigured in the latter."[18] In this radical new conception of the Christian family, everyone gained the ability to become spiritual nobility. The city of God—his kingdom—is populated not by an earthly aristocracy but by the rich hidden lives of people devoted to the glory of God rather than the glory of themselves.

---

[17]   Thomas Howard, *Hallowed Be This House* (Harold Shaw Publishers), pp. 89–90.
[18]   R. V. Young, "In Defense of Patriarchy."

13

The City of God

What will become of the modern City of Man? Having been built on a shallow and shifting foundation, the decadence of the cosmopolitan life has given way, and the pain, disorder, and pathologies have grown impossible to ignore. The chaos and rupture seeded long ago is now laid bare, but despite this barren land, we have been given all that we need to transform it and make it whole once more.

The word *devil* comes from the Greek word *diabolos*, which can be translated "to divide," "to separate," or more literally, "to throw against." At the heart of the woke movement is not unity but rupture—rupture from our shared past, from a shared vocabulary, from an ability to reason together, from a canon of Western philosophy and literature, and from a shared purpose and identity as human beings.

This scattering has severe and far-reaching effects. Globally, we have seen for years a concern over an epidemic of loneliness. There is also an epidemic of woundedness and hurt. There's an irony there, that an impersonal society that degrades and reduces the human person creates people who take everything personally. It is another sign of the way in which we make gods of ourselves, each becoming tyrants of our separate kingdom cells.

We try to patch over these ruptures with be nice campaigns, corporate sermons on consent, and celebrity sing-a-longs to "Imagine." But when life inevitably and suddenly ignites and collapses, we realize the scope of the horror just beneath the surface and the utter insufficiency of our remedies. Flannery O'Connor wrote about this attempt to maintain a kind or tender society without Christ or the Faith. "It is a tenderness which, long cut off from the person of Christ, is wrapped in theory. When tenderness is detached from the source of tenderness, its logical outcome is terror. It ends in forced-labor camps and in the fumes of the gas chamber."[1] A movement which is animated by hatred of the Logos and innocence, if allowed to fester, will end in violence and persecution of Christians. We need courage and a love of Christ and his cross.

We should not delude ourselves about the battle at hand, but even more so should we have confidence in, and clarity about, the immense and gratuitous love of God. The greatest rupture we face is not among friends or within families or societies but that of separation from Christ. As much as there is to bemoan about the state of the world, the suffering in this life is either a weapon that threatens to separate us from him or a path which brings us closer to him. How we endure suffering determines our citizenship in either the City of Man or the City of God. St. Augustine writes,

---

[1]   Flannery O'Connor, *Mystery and manners: Occasional prose* (New York: Farrar, Straus and Giroux, 1974).

"What is really important, then, is not the character of the suffering but rather the character of the sufferer. Stirred by the same motion, filth gives out a foul stench, but perfume a sweet fragrance."[2]

This world begins as a carnival and ends as a reckoning or a reunion. The more committed we are to utopia here, the more elusive it becomes. Without an eternal perspective, we lose sight of even a temporal one.

G. K. Chesterton wrote of this need for an eternal perspective and the fleeting nature of this life. With a merely temporal perspective, we take inequality as a given and argue and battle for equality, all the while believing in our cynical modern way that equality is an illusion.

> In truth it is inequality that is the illusion. The extreme disproportion between men, that we seem to see in life, is a thing of changing lights and lengthening shadows, a twilight full of fancies and distortions. We find a man famous and cannot live long enough to find him forgotten; we see a race dominant and cannot linger to see it decay. . . . It is when men have seen and suffered much and come at the end of more elaborate experiments, that they see men under an equal light of death and daily laughter; and none the less mysterious for being many.[3]

---

2   Augustine, *City of God: Book I* (New York: City Press), p. 8.

3   G. K. Chesterton, in *What I saw in America* (New York: Dodd, Mead and Company, 1922), p. 17.

Body and Spirit

The rupture of the woke movement is fundamentally a crisis of the impending erasure of the human person. We see the beginnings of this with the elevation of a sort of androgynous modern ideal of the human person. The Church, in contrast, prompts us to contend with the whole of the person, without denigrating or deifying him.

We learn something of our existential vulnerability and duty from knowing we begin life as an infant. So too can we learn something essential about who we are by the reality of our biological capacities to father a child or grow life within our bodies. These bodily realities speak to profound spiritual realities which are made trite when reduced to being about tasks and career options.

What our bodies point to is something deeper than biological fatherhood and motherhood. It is not that we must have these biological realities in fact, but in kind. An infertile man does not cease to be a man because of the fact of his infertility. A post-menopausal woman does not cease to be a woman because she is barren. But the person cannot be whole and somehow defined out of these basic bodily capacities.

On a fundamental level, the response of the Church needs to be reclaiming what it means to be a man and to be a woman. Without reclaiming this, we will not know *how* to be familial, nor why we should *want* to. Seeking to restore the person is not for human virtue alone, or for the sake of a well-functioning society, though those things are good. It is also, and more importantly, for rebuilding the Church, which stands immediately antecedent and immediately consequent to the restoration of the person. Whole persons form stronger families who become fertile ground for the Church. Conversely, we need the Church, imbued with authority and courage, to shepherd her flock.

The Priesthood

The fatherhood of the priest is a signpost of these deeper realities at play in our biology. Though not a biological father, he is truly a father. When my sons were young, I was surprised by how much they loved training to be altar servers and assisting at Mass. Upon reflection, it struck me that a significant part of their valuing it was connected to it being exclusively for boys. Had it been for all children, I think it would have seemed like just another children's activity—more of a chore than an honor. Instead, part of what they responded to and understood on some level was that this was not just another childhood thing but a window into becoming a man and a father. There was a certain mystery and reverence elicited from them through the responsibility implicit in it.

The priesthood is not a job that can be negotiated, nor accessed on demand. It is a calling to be an icon of the fatherhood of God and a representation of the incarnate God who became man. That the priesthood is male is not symbolic of women who are not smart enough, holy enough, or of equal dignity but rather a deep recognition that we are all made for family life. Rather than superficial distinctions or referents to tasks, fatherhood and motherhood are icons of deeper, more profound truths.

Without men answering a calling particular to their being men, religion is too easily reduced to a thing of sentiment. It becomes maternal in distorted ways. The icon of fatherhood lends a credence to the reality of spiritual battle and a war against the enemies of Christ. The jettisoning of the authority of God and the Church has, as the revolutionaries plotted, gone by way of the corruption of both biological and spiritual fatherhood. Men who do not see the vital need for them *as men*, fighting for the innocence of children and defending and spreading the Faith, will not see much need for themselves at all. Cut off from their deeper purpose, they drift into contrived ones.

St. Teresa of Calcutta was asked by St. John Paul the Great to write a letter to women. In it she emphasized that we are created for great things—to love and be loved—and that part of that profound truth is reflected in how God made us. "But why did God make some of us men and others women?" she asked. "Because a woman's love is one image of the love of God, and a man's love is another image of God's love. Both are created to love, but each in a different way. Woman and man complete each other, and together show forth God's love more fully than either can do it alone."[4] Her meaning was not fundamentally about men and women *doing* different things but about them *being* different things.

---

4   Claire Dwyer, "A Special Power of Loving: Mother Teresa's Letter on Women," *Even the Sparrow* (blog), September 2, 2020, https://eventhesparrow.com/a-special-power-of-loving-mother-teresas-letter-on-women/.

Without understanding who we are, we cannot discern whom it is we are meant to be. In intimate friendship with Christ, we become ourselves, but denial of our created nature is an obstacle to sincere friendship with our Creator. A man who is domineering or predatory or chauvinistic is in want of manliness, not in excess of it. A woman who scorns her fertility or is ostentatious in her sexuality is deficient in womanliness. Men become more manly with holiness, and women grow womanlier. Not through a thin conception of roles and relegation, but in a deeper way—as symbols and expressions of the nature and love of God.

Our Lady, Queen and Mother

It should come as no surprise that in losing sight of a healthy man / woman dynamic, we have lost sight of not only fatherhood but of the ideal woman as well.

During the iconoclasm and turmoil of the Reformation in Europe, Luther and the reformers determined that the vow of celibacy for religious life was no longer the ideal and should be replaced entirely with an ideal of domesticity. Women who had spent years living in religious communities were forced to abandon their communities and give themselves in marriage to men. While domesticity is good and noble, what was lost was the sense that women were capable of radically devoting their lives to God with the strength and resolve that the celibate life demands. Eliminated from the Christian cultural ideal was the valued role of these women who were visionaries and mystics organizing their lives, running communities, establishing charities, and devoting themselves more deeply to prayer, study, writing, and art.

While Marian devotion did persist in some reformed areas, it was mostly discouraged, resulting in a shift in our understanding of Mary and consequently of womanhood. Amy Wellborn writes, "[Mary] was no longer a powerful intercessor or protector—she was instead, the Reformers preached, a model of domesticity. As the cult of the saints was eliminated, what went with it was the notion that a woman could powerfully serve a community's interest, and could be a role model, guide, and help for women and men."[5]

The cultural and spiritual rhythm of celebrating these women's virtues on their feast days and near their shrines evaporated from the larger culture and became an oddity of Catholics. "Confraternities devoted to Mary, to the Rosary—composed of mostly men—disappeared. In short, in this new world, there seemed to be no place for brilliant, compelling women like Catherine of Siena or Hildegard of Bingen to be revered for their spiritual wisdom."[6] No longer could men and women look to women for protection. Wellborn continues, "From women calling on St. Margaret in the midst of labor, sailors praying the Salve Regina as they launched, Parisians honoring Genevieve who had saved their

5   Amy Welborn, "Women and the Protestant Reformation," *The Catholic World Report*, October 28, 2017, https://www. catholicworldreport.com/2017/10/28/women-and-the-protestant -reformation/.

6   Ibid.

city, Spaniards under the patronage of Teresa of Avila—all of this became inconceivable in this new world."[7]

In short, as our cultural reverence toward women disintegrated in this very specific but fundamental way, so have we set ourselves up for a diminished understanding of the role of women in ways that have left us vulnerable to the distortions of feminism.

Stripped of the honor due to our Lady, all of the Church, men and women, lose not just a figure of womanhood but a robust conception of the Faith itself. In contemplating the hidden movement toward conversion, Chesterton recognized the role Mary played in leading him to Christ and his Church. As he was battling within himself about becoming Catholic, it was the figure of our Lady that stood in his mind throughout, whether he was defending the Catholic Church or disputing against it to others or to himself. "But whether the figure [of Mary] was distant, or was dark and mysterious, or was a scandal to my contemporaries, or was a challenge to myself—I never doubted that this figure was the figure of the Faith; that she embodied, as a complete human being still only human, all that this Thing had to say to humanity." As the supreme recipient of the gratuitous love of God, Chesterton knew that our Lady served as a source of both intrigue and scandal for a non-Catholic. "The instant I remembered the Catholic Church, I remembered her; when I tried to forget the Catholic Church, I tried to forget her; when I finally saw what was nobler than my fate, the freest and the hardest

_____

[7]   Ibid.

of all my acts of freedom, it was in front of a gilded and very gaudy little image of her."[8]

In the Holy Family, we find the blueprint of life. The moment of God's entry into the world was first in the Annunciation and then in the Nativity. Both moments were still and small in the context of family life. Mary received him with a perfect *yes* and became a mother—*the* mother— to her Son, who is the Father of all. Christ was born into this family in the still of the night and in the piercing cold, with torture and death prowling for the innocent Child. The world stood suspended and upended as the heavenly kingdom rejoiced.

We can picture Mary beholding his gaze. We can meditate on Joseph—strong, protective, and gentle—beholding his family. Christ and the first Christians gathered together at the seam of time. Their holiness, and ours, is not found in the extraordinary things but through persevering obedience in the ordinary. But ordinary should not be misconstrued as mediocre. Rather, the same love that called for the simplicity of domesticity also offered the suffering and sorrow of torture and crucifixion.

The serpent hates Mary because she, a creature, is elevated above all the angels and has the power to draw souls to her Son. By receiving Christ, and reverencing, serving, and loving him, she became the most powerful woman in history, past, present, and future. Not through human power does she become powerful but through service. Because he hates her, the devil wants us, men and women, to believe we are

---

[8] G. K. Chesterton, *The Well and the Shallows.*

above the call to serve—not to elevate us but to diminish her. "Ye shall be as gods" is the lie. In the Holy Family, the cross, and the Resurrection, we find the truth.

The City

The battle is not a political one. It is a spiritual one. We can be confident that in bleak times there are the stirrings of great longing for eternal things. On a recent trip to San Francisco, I was struck by how much it's a study in extremes: incredible wealth juxtaposed with rampant destitution, a sky-scraping metropolis on the precipice of a horizon of wild ocean. Even walking the steep city hills will remind you that there's little space here for middle ground. A city that publicly celebrates pride rather than humility couldn't have a more needed patron than St. Francis, who left a life of wealth and prestige to live humbly in both circumstance and soul.

Despite visiting San Francisco all my life, I did not remember the poverty and cultural disorientation being so extreme. Now the city seems rough and pregnant with dread. It might be a bit easier to become inured to it all as a resident, or at least not to feel the punch of sadness of it all, but for a visitor, it feels a bit like walking through tragedy. What begins in decadence ends in violence.

During our time there, we visited a local church. The liturgy was fine, the sacrament was transformative, the priest said something vaguely heretical. In other words, a common Mass experience in modern America.

It's easy to become blasé about all this: the wealth and destitution, the miracle and the heresy. So much of the spiritual life is seeing beyond the everyday so as not to drown in the complacency of a comfortable evil or become indifferent to a transformative grace. Surfaces are deceiving; we forget that there is an abyss of evil and mountains of grace, and the extremes exist not just visibly in a city but very painfully inside our Church.

In many ways, it's an old tale. In his imaginings of hell, Dante reserves some of the lowest levels for bishops and priests. The Church has always been a battleground for all people at all stages of the spiritual life, from St. Francis to Oscar Wilde, Chris Farley to Andy Warhol. All creatures, saints and sinners, struggling, resisting, revolting, and returning over and over until their last breath.

There is something intangible that we can sense in people who have suffered much, but suffered well, united to the cross. They share a common characteristic of lightness—not in a superficially sunny way but a lightness born of great depth. They reflect Christ back to us so that we might grow in love for Christ. They are light, and in that light, we see him.

In a letter to a friend, Flannery O'Connor wrote about the hope and dread she felt as a Catholic living in modern times. "I think that the Church is the only thing that is going to make the terrible world we are coming to endurable; the only thing that makes the Church endurable is that it is somehow the body of Christ and that on this we are fed."[9] She looked at the everyday and saw disfigurement and

---

[9]   Ralph C. Wood, *Flannery O'Connor and the Christ-Haunted South* (Wm. B. Eerdmans, 2005).

grace. We can be tempted to look at disfigurement and grace and see the everyday.

The horizon of eternity stretches before us. There's no space here for middle ground between the devil and Christ. Both are hard at work for souls—one by subversion, the other by light. Each of us, the religious and the layman, the priest and the pope, must serve one or the other. "No one can serve two masters," Christ reminds us. Let the light be relentless, revealing in its clarity (sometimes painfully so), and awakening us to the reality that the stakes are high and the risk eternal.

Shortly before she died, St. Monica and her son St. Augustine enjoyed a heartfelt conversation about eternal things. For years, her prayers, steadfast and fervent, had helped sustain the seed of faith in her beloved son, culminating in the joy of his prodigious return to Christ. In this moment, in what turned out to be her last days, they sat speaking of the eternal city, the fabric separating them from that city seemingly thin and insignificant. The conversation was somewhat mystical, a glimpse into an unspeakable joy with Christ that they shared with one another as fellow pilgrims traveling to be with him there.

And somehow in that longing for that city we catch a glimpse of it—not in the machinery of the city of man but in the wide landscape of the city of God. One is steel and cement; the other is field and forest.

"Let us pine for the City where we are citizens. . . . By pining, we are already there; we have already cast our hope, like an anchor, on that coast. I sing of somewhere else, not of here; for I sing with my heart, not my flesh. The citizens of Babylon hear the sound of the flesh, the Founder of Jerusalem hears the tune of the heart."[10]

---

[10] A Sermon from Saint Augustine of Hippo in Peter Brown, *Augustine of Hippo,* p. 314.